KARAKURIDÔJI
ULTIMO

WHAT?

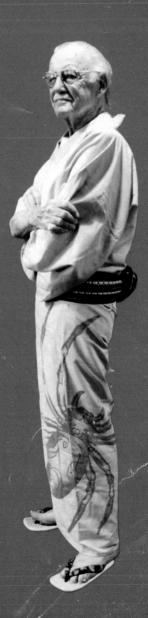

Stan Lee's POW! Entertainment
Takei
SHONEN JUMP MANG
KARAKURIDÔJI
ULTIMO
original concept: STAN LEE
story and art by: HIROYUKI TAKEI
inker: DAIGO
painter: BOB
1

KARAKURIDÔJI

ULTIMO 1

C O N T E N T S

霊 HEART IS WHERE THE *SPIRIT* OF GOOD OR EVIL LIES.

剣 SUPERIOR STRENGTH IS A *SWORD* THAT MANIFESTS ONE'S WILL.

鏡 PUPPETS ARE *MIRRORS* THAT REFLECT MORE THAN THEIR HUMAN CREATORS.

ACT 1 NANBAN-OKINA PASS

ACT 1
NANBAN-OKINA PASS

KARAKURIDÔJI

ULTIMO

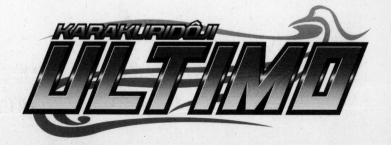

12th century

KYOTO
Japan

RATTLE *RATTLE* *RATTLE* *RATTLE*

RATTLE *RATTLE* *RATTLE*

...

WAIT, OLD MAN.

RATTLE

YES?
WHO IS THIS GUY?!
GAH

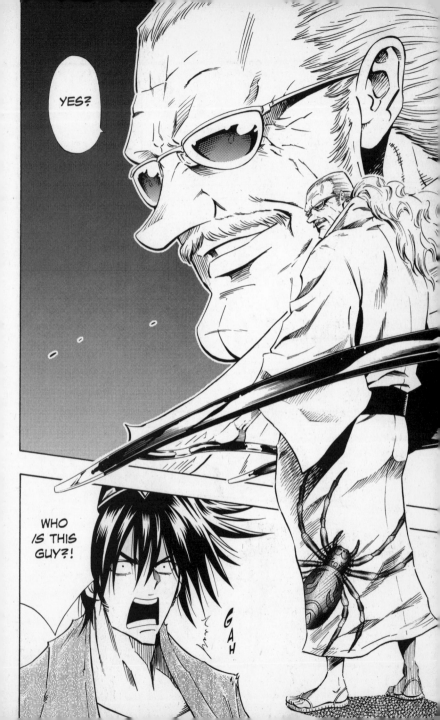

TCH! YOU'RE ODD, OLD MAN. WHO ARE YOU?
MY NAME IS DUNSTAN.
WHUMP
DUNSTAN...? A FOREIGNER. ARE YOU A NANBAN TRADER HEADED FOR THE CAPITAL?
WHAT A LUXURIOUS CART. THE GOODS INSIDE MUST BE GIFTS FOR THE HIGH NOBILITY.
THEY MIGHT BE.
AND WHO ARE YOU?
I'M YAMATO.
HEH
I'M A BANDIT.

DON'T TRY TO RUN IF YOU WANT TO LIVE.

HEH HEH...

SORRY, OLD MAN. WE'RE GOING TO HAVE YOU LEAVE THOSE WITH US.

RUSTLE

WE WON'T KILL YOU IF YOU DON'T START ANY TROUBLE.

STRANGE BANDITS.

SUCH UNNEC- ESSARY NUMBERS. OLD MEN AND EVEN CHILDREN!

HA!

YOU REALLY OUGHT NOT TO TOUCH *THESE*...
I HAVE CREATED THEM. THEY ARE EQUAL TO EACH OTHER. NOTHING LIKE THEM HAS EVER EXISTED.
VICE
THEY ARE *ULTIMATE* MECHANICAL BOYS. FIVE SENSES REACH INTO FIVE DIMENSIONS AND FOUR LIMBS EXTEND INTO FOUR DIMENSIONS. THAT ADDS UP TO THE POWER OF NINE DIMENSIONS.
IF YOU WAKE THEM, YOU *WILL* ALL DIE.
OH, REALLY?
!
SHING

THEIR SHODDY GOVERNMENT HAS COST US OUR HOMES, OUR FAMILIES...

SORRY, BUT I DON'T CARE *WHAT* YOU'VE GOT.

WE HATE THE NOBILITY.

FROM NOW ON, WE'RE TAKING IT ALL BACK.

WE ARE HERE TO MAKE SURE THEY CAN'T HAVE ANYTHING ELSE.

I SEE. YOU'RE *DUTY BANDITS.*

DRIP

VICE

BUT THEY ARE *ULTIMATE GOOD* AND *EVIL.*

ULTIMO

AND WHILE DUTY BANDITS MAY IN ESSENCE BE WORKING FOR THE GREATER GOOD, *EVIL* IS *EVIL*.
GOOD WON'T FORGIVE YOU. AND NO AMOUNT OF REASONING WILL WORK ON *EVIL*.
IF YOU WANT TO PROTECT YOURSELVES...
...IT'S ALL THE MORE REASON YOU SHOULDN'T DO ANYTHING SO FOOLISH AS TO UNDO THE ROPE ON THESE BOXES AND OPEN THE LIDS.
...?!
BOSS...?
HUBBUB
DON'T BE AFRAID!

KEH! THE OLD MAN'S BLUFFING!
ULTIMATE GOOD AND EVIL?
YOU AN IDIOT? NOTHING IS ULTIMATE OR GOOD OR EVIL. YOU'VE GOT IT ALL WRONG.
BUT YOU TALK SO MUCH... YOU MUST HAVE SOMETHING VALUABLE IN THERE.
SMIRK
ALL RIGHT, MEN.
I SAY OPEN UP THE BOXES RIGHT NOW.
SMIRK
YES!
SMIRK
ONE... TWO...

...
ULTIMO
VICE
D...
DOLLS ...?

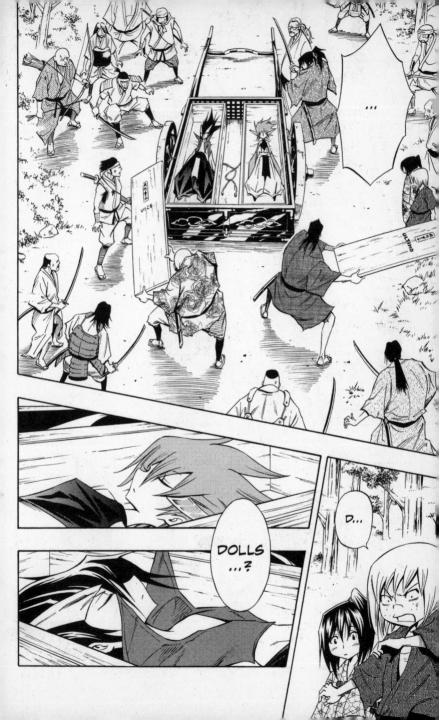

HA HA HA! I THOUGHT SOMETHING WOULD LEAP OUT AT ME. BUT THEY'RE JUST DOLLS!
I *KNEW* YOU WERE JUST BLUFFING, YOU TRICKY OLD MAN!
...
B...
BUT, BOSS...
... THESE ARE REALLY FINE GOODS.
THE SKIN IS WHITE AND SMOOTH LIK CERAMIC.
THE CLOTHES HAVE BEEN WOVEN FROM HIGH-QUALITY FABRIC, AND THEY SPARKLE.
AND THE GAUNTLETS HAVE BEEN DYED IN MULTIPLE LAYERS AND GIVE OUT A RICH COLOR!
NO MATTER WHERE I LOOK, IT'S FIRST-CLASS CRAFTSMANSHIP SUCH AS I'VE NEVER SEEN.
BESIDES, MORE THAN ANYTHING ELSE...

...SUCH INCREDIBLE BEAUTY, LIKE A CHERUB...

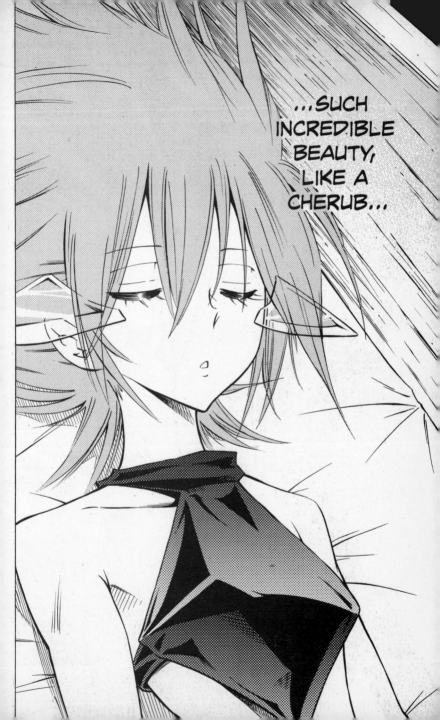

...SUCH INCREDIBLE STRENGTH, LIKE A BRAVE AND GALLANT HERO!!!

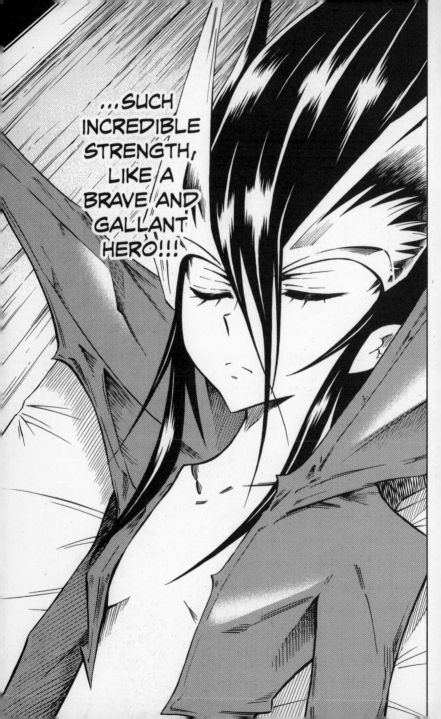

WE COULD GET A GOOD PRICE FOR THESE!
CHATTER
THEY LOOK LIKE THEY'LL START MOVING ON THEIR OWN AT ANY MOMENT!
CHATTER
SO PRETTY ...
THEY LOOK REAL.
HOW NICE, HUH, OLD MAN? YOUR DOLLS HAVE MADE A GOOD IMPRES-SION.
HA HA HA! WHAT AN HONOR!
HOW-EVER...
...THEY'RE NOT DOLLS. THEY'RE MECHANICAL BOYS.
HUH?
WELL, YOU'VE GONE AND OPENED THE FORBIDDEN BOXES.
THEY WILL NOW BE AWAKENED AND BEGIN TO FULFILL THEIR DESTINIES.
ULTIMO...
!

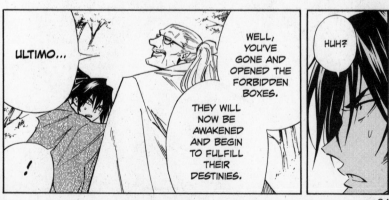

WHAT...
BLINK
...DO YOU THINK OF HIM?
ITS EYES OPENED!
STARE

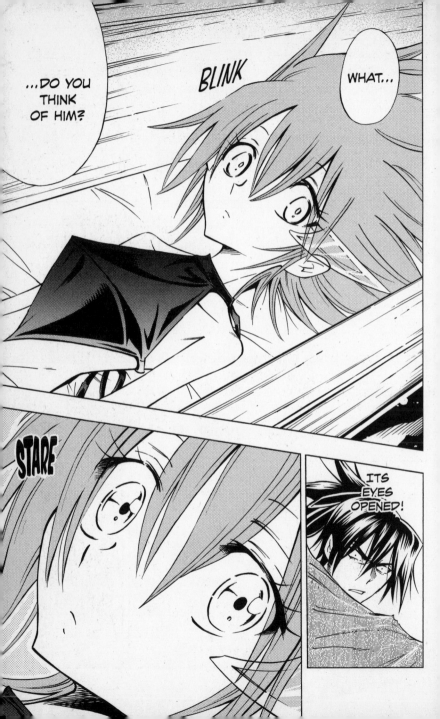

DR. DUNSTAN...
...
LOOKING BACK THROUGH HIS MEMORIES, HE HASN'T DONE ANYTHING THAT EVIL.
GIVEN WHAT'S HAPPENED TO HIM, THERE'S PLENTY OF ROOM FOR LENIENCY.
STILL, HE'S A LITTLE TOO VIOLENT TO BE ULTI'S MASTER.

GAAAAAH! THE DOLL SPEAKS AND MOVES AND EVEN CRITICIZES!
WAAAAAGH
I TOLD YOU NOT TO BE AFRAID!
UGH
INSANE OLD MAN! WHAT ARE YOU UP TO?
YOU KEEP CHILDREN IN BOXES?
...
CHILDREN?
NO, THEY LOOKED LIKE DOLLS...
SURELY YOU WEREN'T GOING TO GIVE THESE CHILDREN TO THE NOBILITY... WERE YOU?
DON'T BE STUPID.
RUSTLE

I'M NOT A KID OR A DOLL.
I AM A KARAKURI DÔJI! A MECHANICAL BOY!
AND I DO NOT WISH TO BE AWAKENED BY THE LIKES OF YOU!
YOU ANGER ME. FOR THAT, YOU DIE!
TWITCH TWITCH

THWAK
THWAK
THWAK
THWAK
NO MORE MESSING AROUND, BOSS. SOMETHING'S WRONG WITH THOSE DOLLS!
TREMBLE
TREMBLE
TREMBLE
THOSE ARE CLAWS, SOME KIND OF WEAPONS!
NOW THE RED ONE. GET EVERYBODY OUTTA HERE FAST! PLEASE!
TH...
THE RED ONE?
FOOL! YOU ACT ONLY ON MY ORDER!

OUR ENEMY IS THE NOBILITY!
WE DON'T ATTACK CHILDREN!
I TOLD YOU, I'M NOT A KID!
TIME TO LISTEN, FOOL!

HEH HEH... YOU CAN HAVE THESE BACK.
THUD
HUH ...?
IT'S ALIVE...
EVEN THOUGH ALL THOSE ARROWS HIT IT!
GYAAAAAH! IT'S NOT HUUUU...
FWSH

HRAAAH!!!
SLASH
IT JUMPED...?
HE KNOCKED THEM UP TO THE TOP OF THE TREE WITH ONE KICK...
AND THOSE CLAWS... NO, WHAT'S WORSE...

...IT'S FLYING.
NOW...
...FOR THE OTHER THREE FOOLS WHO FIRED ARROWS AT ME.
DOWN BELOW, SEVEN MA AWAY, ONE HIDES IN THE SHADOWS.
UP ABOVE, 12 MA AWAY, TWO HIDE IN THE BRANCHES.
ANNOYING. I'LL JUST TAKE THEM ALL OUT FROM UP HERE.

SHOOM
UGK...
GAH!
GASP...

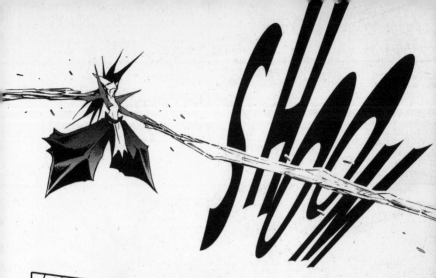

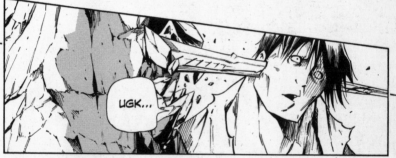

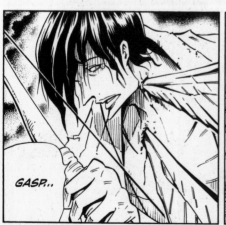

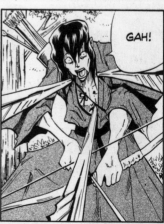

HEH HEH!
KLAK
KLAK
KLAK
IT'S JUST NOT ENOUGH YET.
MUST KILL THE IDIOT WHO WOKE ME.
NO.
SUCH SMALL NUMBERS WILL NOT SATISFY MY HANNYA PARA-METERS.
SNAP
MUST KILL *EVERYONE*.
POP POP

I'LL ...
KLAK
... CUT ...
POP
... EVERY-ONE...
KLAK KLAK KLAK
...100 TIMES EACH!

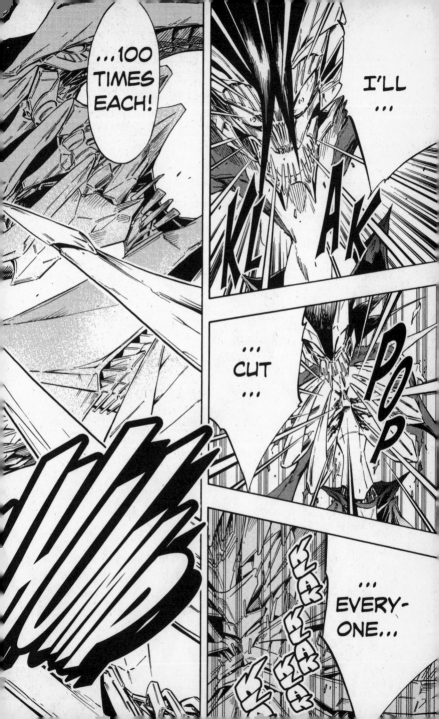

KARAKURI HENGE! ONI MEN!! DEMON MASK!!!

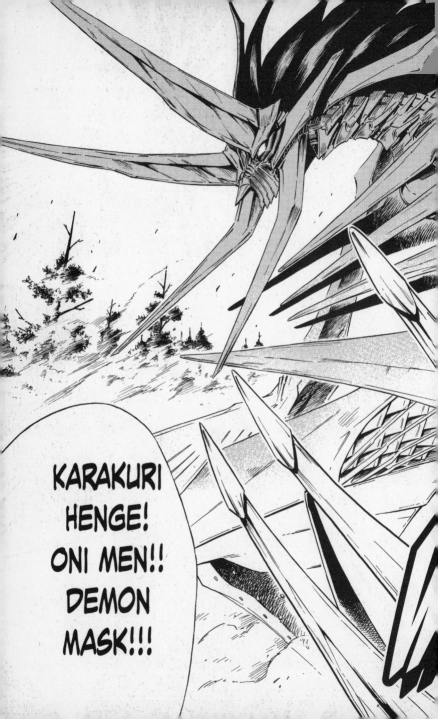

WHAT'S HAPPENING?
THIS CHILD...
THE OLD MAN...
ULTIMATE... GOOD... EVIL...
NONE OF THAT MATTERS...
MY PEOPLE...
...ARE DEAD...

YOU!
THUMP
!
YOU.
YOU'RE THE FOOL WHO WOKE ME.
YOU'LL BE LAST. FIRST WATCH AS I KILL YOUR COMPANIONS.
NYAH!
YIIIIIKES!
I WON'T LET YOU.

I WILL STOP YOU.
YOU WILL BE PUNISHED.
A CHILD IS NO MATCH FOR ME!

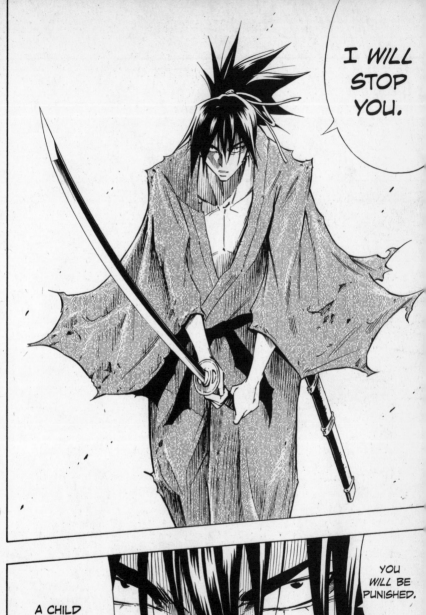

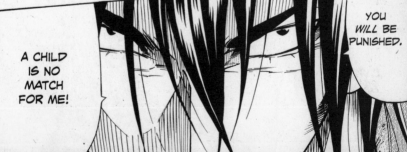

BOSS...

B...

YOU MAY BE A FOOL, BUT YOU ARE NOT A COWARD.

HUH?

YOU SAY THIS EVEN AFTER WATCHING ME WORK?

I'LL FIGHT TOO.
'CAUSE I OPENED ONE OF THE BOXES.
SHING
HUUH?!
HOW ARE YOU GOING TO FIGHT AGAINST *THAT*?!
!
WELL, AREN'T YOU ASKING YOURSELF THE SAME THING?
YOU DON'T GO AT THIS ALONE. NOT GONNA HAPPEN.
WE'RE BETTER IF WE ACT TOGETHER!
SHING

I'LL FIGHT TOO.
SIX OF OUR COMRADES ARE DEAD.
WE HAVE NO CHOICE.
EVEN IF I RAN, WHERE WOULD I GO?
...
THIS IS MY HOME.
IT'S STRANGE, BUT I'M NOT AFRAID!
IT DOESN'T SEEM REAL.
LIVING LIKE THIS EVERY DAY IS MORE TERRIFYING THAN THAT BOY.
YOU FOOLS...
HEY BOSS, WHAT ABOUT THE AMAZING KARAKURI DÔJI?

I DON'T KNOW HOW THOSE DOLLS WORK, BUT WE'RE BANDITS, RIGHT?
IF WE STOLE THAT ONE FOR OUR SIDE, WE COULD EASILY BEAT THE NOBILITY.
BESIDES, SHE SAYS SHE WANTS IT.
'CAUSE IT'S PRETTY.
NOD
YOU MUSTN'T...
BLOOP
NO! JUST GET OUT OF HERE!
HEY!
WHUMP

I'M...
...AMAZED...
...AT YOUR RIDICULOUS SHOW OF LOYALTY. IT ANGERS ME.
!
I'M GOING TO KILL YOU NOW.
KARAKURI HENGE!
SHISHI GUCHI!! MOUTH OF THE LION!!!

SHISHI-MAI! DANCE OF THE LION!!
...!
...!

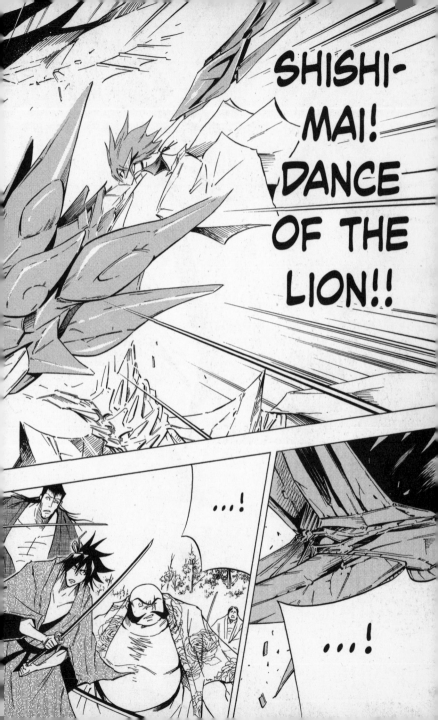

WHACK
-tweet-

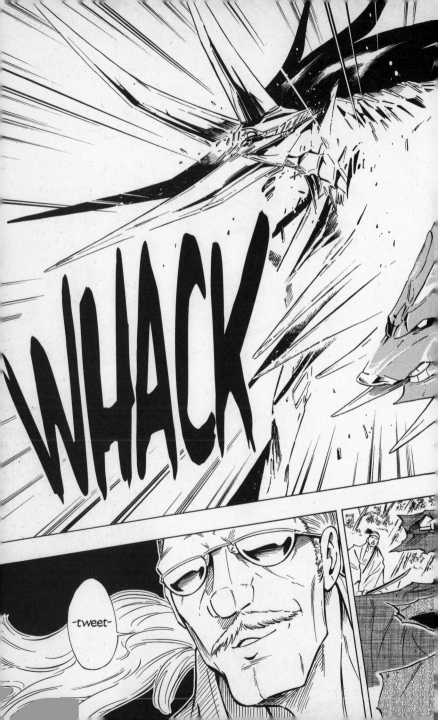

VICE. ENOUGH.
HUNH?!
THE RED ONE HELPED ME?
YOU ALREADY KILLED SIX.
KLAK KLAK KLAK
I WILL NOT ALLOW ANY MORE MEANINGLESS SLAUGHTER.
KLAK
NO MORE OF THEM...
KLAK KLAK KLAK KLAK

...OR I WILL BREAK YOU.
HEH HEH.
WELL, NOW...
KLAK
KLAK
KLAK
KLAK
WHEN DID YOU TAKE THE SIDE OF BANDITS?

ULTIMO!!
SHO
M
KARAKURI HENGE! KOGUCHI!!
MOUTH OF THE FOX!!
IT'S NO USE, VICE.
!
CHAK
I KNOW YOUR EVERY MOVE. YOUR ATTACKS WON'T WORK ON ME.

IT IS WRONG TO STEAL...
...BUT THEY SHOW STEADFAST SENTIMENT TOWARD THEIR COMRADES.
AND SENTI-MENT...
...IS THE HEART OF *GOODNESS* AND DOESN'T DESERVE TO BE KILLED.
BE QUIET!
I'M *EVIL*. YOU THINK I CARE?
H...

HEY! WHAT'S GOING ON, OLD MAN? THEY'RE FIGHTING EACH OTHER!
OF COURSE.
THEY ARE *ULTIMATE GOOD* AND *EVIL*. THEY DO NOT MIX, LIKE WATER AND OIL.
WHAT DID YOU THINK WOULD HAPPEN IF YOU WOKE THEM UP TOGETHER?
NO ONE CAN STOP THEM NOW.
NOT EVEN I.
EVERYONE WILL DIE.
A SERIOUS BATTLE BETWEEN THEM WILL LEAVE NOTHING BUT WASTE BEHIND.
HUH?!
I DO NOT WISH TO STOP THEM.
THE SOLE REASON I MADE THEM...
...WAS TO KNOW WHICH IS STRONGER, *GOOD* OR *EVIL*.

I AM A SCHOLAR. I'VE LONG SOUGHT THE ULTIMATE STRENGTH.
BUT THE OBSTACLE TO THAT HAS ALWAYS BEEN... GOOD AND EVIL.
HUMANS, WHICH SHOULD BE THE STRONGEST CREATURES ON EARTH, ARE AT THE MERCY OF THESE TWO CONFLICTING ELEMENTS WITHIN THEM, AND THUS LOSE THEIR STRENGTH.
...EVEN THOUGH TIME OR PLACE TEACH HUMANS DIFFERENTLY AND THERE'S NO CLEAR DEFINITION NOR SHAPE TO GOOD AND EVIL.
STRANGE, YET FRUSTRATING, EH?
LOOM
THE WORLD VIEWS THE ACTIONS OF BANDITS AS EVIL, BUT TO THE GOOD AUTHORITIES THOSE ACTIONS ARE ACTUALLY TRIFLING.
BECAUSE THEY STEAL SEVERAL THOUSAND TIMES MORE FROM PEOPLE IN ORDER TO LINE THEIR OWN POCKETS.
!
...!
SO WHAT SEPARATES GOOD AND EVIL? WHETHER PEOPLE ACCEPT THEM OR NOT? NO.
THE ANSWERS TO WHY PEOPLE LIVE IN CHAINS LIE DEEPER WITHIN THEIR HUMAN SOULS.

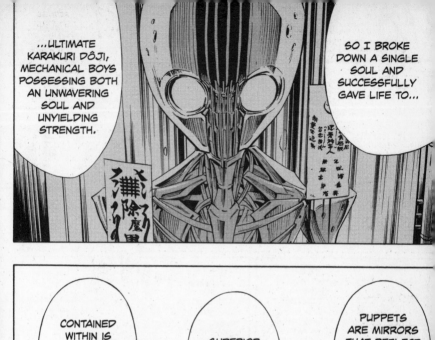

SO I BROKE DOWN A SINGLE SOUL AND SUCCESSFULLY GAVE LIFE TO...
...ULTIMATE KARAKURI DÔJI, MECHANICAL BOYS POSSESSING BOTH AN UNWAVERING SOUL AND UNYIELDING STRENGTH.
PUPPETS ARE MIRRORS THAT REFLECT MUCH MORE THAN THEIR HUMAN CREATORS.
SUPERIOR STRENGTH IS A *SWORD* THAT MANIFESTS ONE'S WILL.
CONTAINED WITHIN IS THE PURE *SPIRIT* OF GOOD OR EVIL.

ACROSS TIME AND SPACE, THE KARAKURI DŌJI WILL SERVE MANY MASTERS, LEARN THOSE THREE TRUTHS, AND IN DUE COURSE THEY WILL HAVE THEIR FINAL BATTLE.
WHICH WILL WIN, *GOOD* OR *EVIL*? WHAT INFLUENCE WILL THE RESULT HAVE OVER HUMANITY?
INTER-ESTING...
...WOULDN'T YOU AGREE?
I DON'T...
...UNDER-STAND!
THE STRONGEST BEING? WHY WOULD YOU DO THIS?
I UNDERSTAND ONLY THIS.
NOTHING GOOD CAN COME FROM LETTING A CRAZY OLD MAN LIKE YOU LIVE.

H...
HE'S GONE?!
HA HA HA HA! NOW THEIR TRUE FIGHT BEGINS!
!
I LOOK FORWARD TO SEEING HOW YOU FARE IN ALL THIS--YOU WHO OPENED THE BOXES!
DADUM
ULTIMO.
I DO NOT DIE.
FWSH
?!!

THIS IS THE END FOR YOU.
NO, FOR YOU, VICE.
FLASH
...

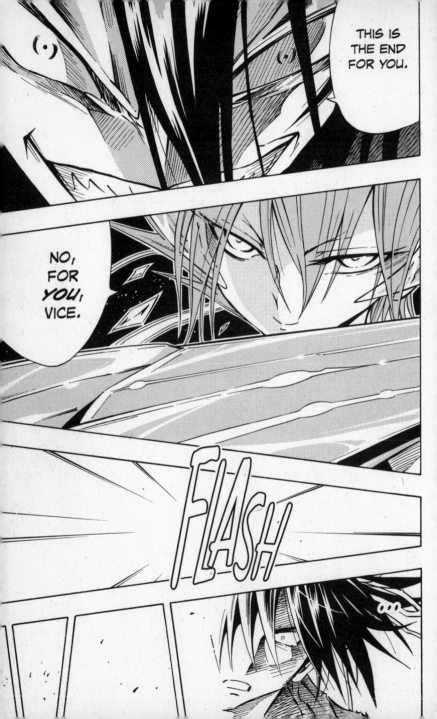

GOOD MORNING, YAMATO!
AS TALL AS EVER!
YOUR HEIGHT ALWAYS GIVES YOU AWAY!
WHAM
AAGH?!

21st century
WEST TOKYO Japan
DCC
HUH? OH, RUNE? YOU'RE AWFULLY ENERGETIC FOR SO EARLY IN THE MORNING.

DID SOMETHING GOOD HAPPEN?
AW, MAN! DID YOU FORGET?
THE BIRTHDAY PARTY'S TONIGHT.
YOU WERE ALL EXCITED ABOUT GIVING SAYAMA A PRESENT.
PUSH
FWUMP
GAH!
HOW DID I FORGET?

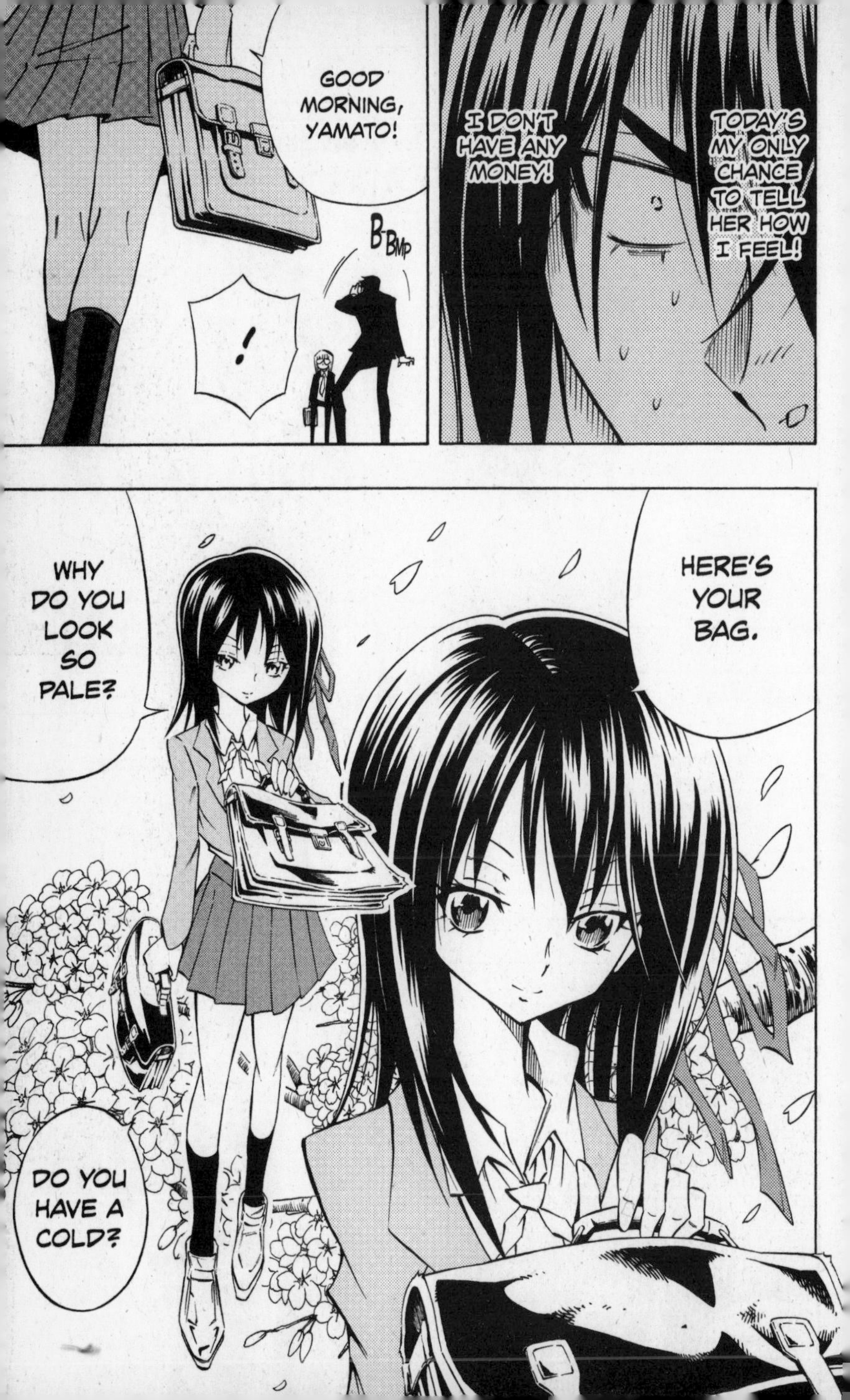
TODAY'S MY ONLY CHANCE TO TELL HER HOW I FEEL!
I DON'T HAVE ANY MONEY!
GOOD MORNING, YAMATO!
B-BMP
!
HERE'S YOUR BAG.
WHY DO YOU LOOK SO PALE?
DO YOU HAVE A COLD?

S- SAYAMA!
SHE'S SO BEAUTIFUL!
BADUMP
I HOPE YOU AREN'T SICK. SO YOU CAN COME TO MY PARTY...
NO, NO, I'LL BE THERE! I'M JUST NOT A MORNING PERSON!
CHAK
YOU'RE WEIRD.
BUT I'M GLAD YOU CAN COME.
CAN'T WAIT TO SEE WHAT YOU BRING.
YEAH!
UNH, I LIKE HER SO MUCH!
SO... WHAT *WILL* YOU BRING?
I'LL TELL YOU RIGHT NOW, I DON'T HAVE ENOUGH MONEY ON ME TO LEND YOU ANY...
WHAT SHOULD I DO? HOW DID I TOTALLY FORGET, RUNE?
I HAVE NO IDEA.
NEITHER DO I!

古美術・刀剣
国分堂
骨董・版画
古物高価買取
HM?
THE KOKUBUNDO SHOPPE...?
AN ANTIQUE SHOP?
I GUESS I JUST HAVE TO PAWN SOMETHING FOR CASH.
RATTLE RATTLE
Excuse me...
YAMATO?!
YOUR SCHOOL-BAG!

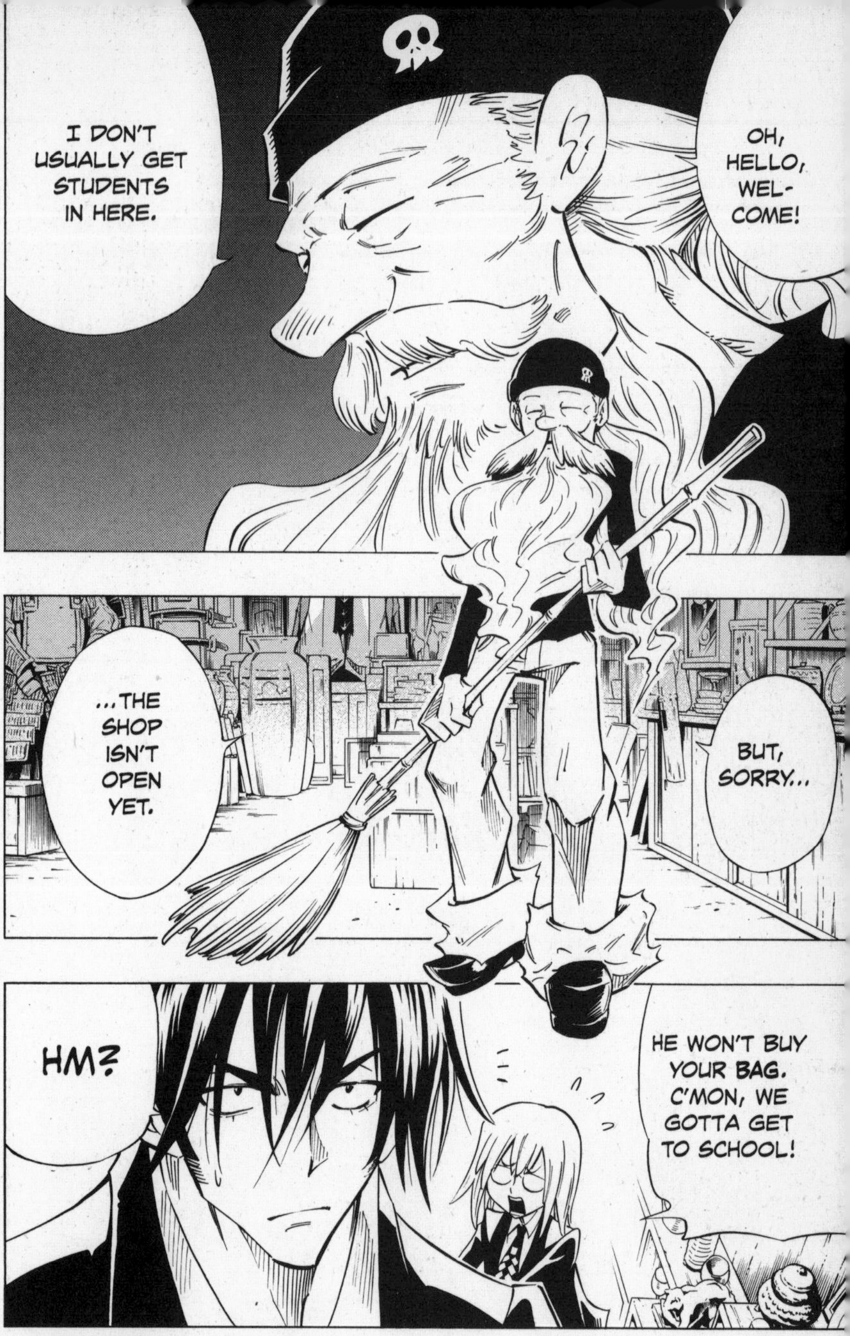
OH, HELLO, WEL-COME!
I DON'T USUALLY GET STUDENTS IN HERE.
BUT, SORRY...
...THE SHOP ISN'T OPEN YET.
HE WON'T BUY YOUR BAG. C'MON, WE GOTTA GET TO SCHOOL!
HM?

ULTIMO?!

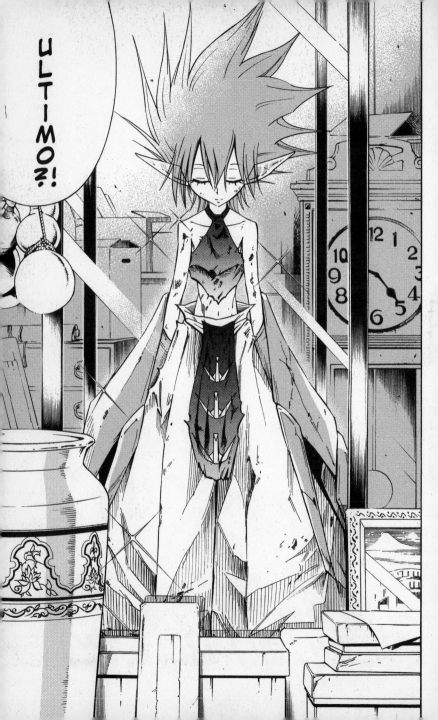

KARAKURIDÔJI
ULTIMO

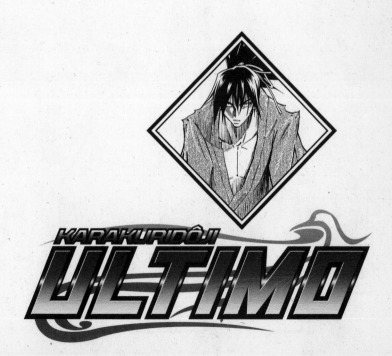

ULTIMO?!

ACT 2: KURENAI DÔJI

ULTIMO?

?

ULTIMO?

WHAT...

...IS ULTIMO, RUNE?
I DON'T KNOW!
DABOOOM
HEY, WHAT'S GOING ON? YOU'RE REALLY WEIRD TODAY, YAMATO!
IT JUST POPPED OUT OF MY HEAD...
UM, WORDS LIKE THAT DON'T JUST POP OUT OF YOUR HEAD!

ま
I ♥ 機巧
ACT 2
KURENAI DÔJI

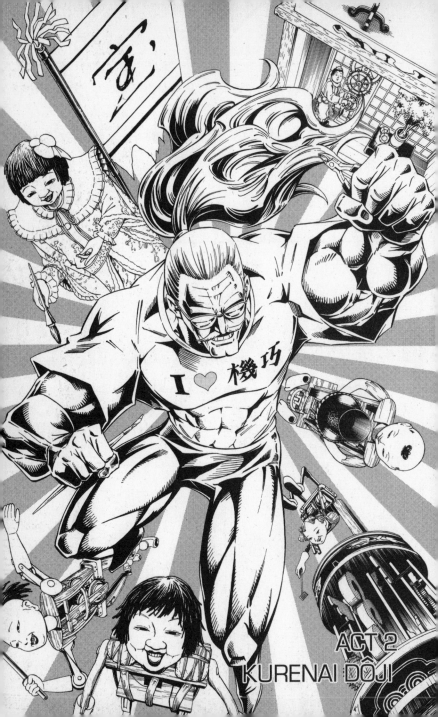

LOOK AT THOSE GAUNT-LETS ...!
HEY GRAMPS, WHAT'S THIS BIG PUPPET GUY CALLED?
I HAVE NO IDEA.
I'VE BEEN SELLING ANTIQUES FOR YEARS, BUT I'VE NEVER SEEN ANYTHING LIKE IT.
I DID SOME RESEARCH, BUT I CAN'T FIGURE OUT WHAT IT'S MADE OF OR WHAT ITS TIME PERIOD IS, MUCH LESS WHAT IT'S CALLED.
I FOUND IT IN THE MOUNTAINS.
YOU *FOUND* IT?!
HA HA HA! OLD MAN FINDS A PUPPET ON THE MOUNTAIN. LIKE A FAIRY TALE!
INDEED!

JUDGING FROM THE CRATER...
...THIS CHILD FELL FROM THE SKY.
SERIOUS? WOW!
NO WAY!
ANYWAY, YOU CAN'T JUST PUT SOMETHING YOU FIND LIKE THAT IN YOUR STORE!
HO HO! WHAT'S WRONG WITH KEEPING WHAT I FIND?
YOU'D UNDERSTAND IF YOU SAW THAT MOUNTAIN.
IT'S COVERED IN TRASH. I'M JUST TRYING TO CLEAN IT UP A LITTLE.

PEOPLE TODAY DON'T TAKE CARE OF ANYTHING.
ONLY LAWS *ARE* GETTING STRICTER. FOOLS THINK AS LONG AS NO ONE FINDS OUT, IT DOESN'T MATTER WHAT THEY DO.
LOOK AT THIS SHOP.
I PICKED OUT ALL THESE TREASURES WITH MY OWN EYES AND GATHERED THEM ALL HERE ON MY OWN.
YOU SHOULDN'T RELY ON OTHERS TO HELP YOU DETERMINE WHAT'S ***GOOD*** AND WHAT'S ***BAD***.
IN NO TIME AT ALL, YOU'LL SIMPLY BE UNDER SOMEONE ELSE'S CONTROL.

GRAMPS...
FELL FROM THE SKY! THAT'S REALLY SOMETHING!
YOU'RE NOT EVEN LISTENING!
WHY WOULDN'T THE NEWS REPORT SOMETHING SO CRAZY?
BLINK
MASTER ...
BLOOP

NINE CENTURIES, YAMATO-SAMA!
KRASSH

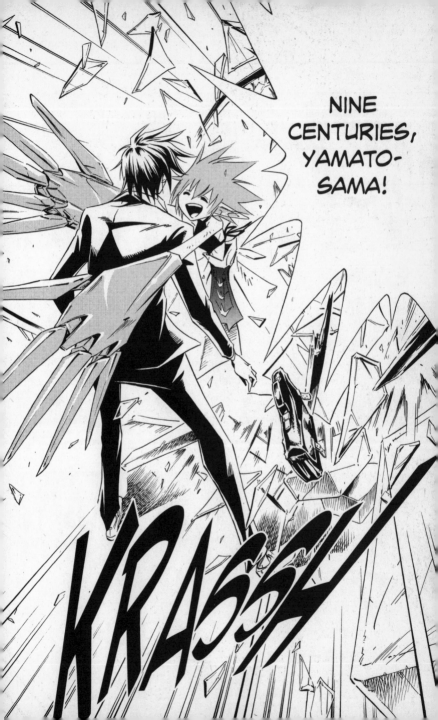

ULTIMO MISSED YOU VERY MUCH!

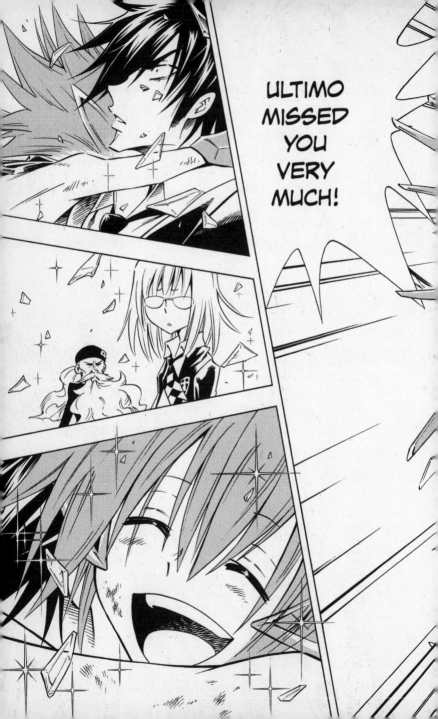

IT TALKED!
IT MOVED!
GLASS!
SHNK
WAP
WHO ARE YOU?!
WHY'S THIS KID IN A GLASS CASE?!
!
BLOOP
HUH ...?
DID MASTER FORGET ABOUT ULTI?
...
DID YOU FORGET THE DAY WE BOUND OURSELVES TOGETHER? WHEN YOU BECAME ULTI'S MASTER AND ULTI BECAME YOUR SERVANT?

WHOA...
YAMATO, WHAT'S HE TALKING ABOUT...?
YOU THINK I HAVE ANY IDEA?!
HOW LONG HAVE YOU KNOWN ME, RUNE?!
THEN...
...WHO IS THIS BOY?
WHO IS THIS BOY?!
WHO'S THIS BOY?!
SHLUMP
I UNDER-STAND.
IT WOULD HAVE BEEN A MIRACLE FOR YOU TO BE REINCARNATED AND STILL REMEMBER ULTI'S NAME.
REINCAR-NATED?!
YES.
WITHOUT A DOUBT YOU ARE THE YAMATO WHO I MET IN THE 12TH CENTURY.

BECAUSE THE SOURCE OF POWER FOR KARAKURI DÔJI SUCH AS ULTI IS THEIR PLEDGE OF DEVOTION TO THEIR LORD AND MASTER.
THAT'S THE ONLY RESTRICTION PLACED ON WE WHO WERE MADE TO BE ULTIMATE GOOD AND EVIL.
UNTIL WE LEARN EVERYTHING FROM OUR MASTER, WE ARE TO OBEY HIM, PROTECT HIM, AND FIGHT ONLY FOR HIM.
AT THE VERY LEAST, WHAT I CAN SAY FOR CERTAIN NOW...
...IS THAT ULTI WOKE UP BECAUSE YOU CAME WITHIN HIS RANGE.

YOUR RANGE?!
I WOULD LOVE TO TALK IT OVER AT LEISURE...
...BUT RIGHT NOW I HAVE URGENT NEWS.
VICE HAS APPEARED IN THIS TIME PERIOD.
VICE...?
ULTI'S OPPOSITE.
A KARAKURI DÔJI OF EVIL WHO LIKES DESTRUCTION AND CARNAGE.
YES.

YAMATO-SAMA'S ORDERS DROVE VICE AWAY. THE GRUDGE HE BEARS KNOWS NO END.
HE FLED FOR HIS LIFE ACROSS TIME AND SPACE, AND YOU FOLLOWED. NOW WITH YOU REINCARNATED IN THE HERE AND NOW, WITHOUT A DOUBT, HE WILL COME FOR YOU.
HE WILL INDEED BE HIDING SOMEWHERE NEARBY ALREADY.
IF WE DON'T FIND AND DEFEAT HIM BEFORE HE FINDS A MASTER AND REGAINS HIS POWER...
...YAMATO-SAMA AND THIS ENTIRE WORLD WILL MEET A TERRIBLE FATE.

SO, YAMATO-SAMA...
...WE MUST RENEW OUR PLEDGE OF DEVOTION, AND TOGETHER DEFEAT VICE!
PLEDGE?!
DEVOTION?!
...
UM... BOY?

I'M SORRY, BUT...
...I NEED TO CONCENTRATE ON WHAT'S IMPORTANT, WHICH IS GETTING A PRESENT FOR SAYAMA.
I'VE HAD...
...A CRUSH ON HER SINCE ELEMENTARY SCHOOL. I CAN'T SCREW THIS UP.
High School
Junior High
Elementary School

I DON'T KNOW WHAT KIND OF GAME THIS KARAWHATSIT DOSOMETHING IS, BUT YOU SHOULDN'T BREAK GLASS.
YOU'RE CAUSING TROUBLE. YOU'RE DRESSED FUNNY...
RIGHT?
YAMATO-SAMA...
WHOOSH
AND YOU, GRAMPS!
!
HUHN
WHAT ARE YOU THINKING?!
BEFORE YOU PLAY WITH YOUR GRANDCHILD, GET YOUR *OWN* ACT TOGETHER!
REALLY...
...I JUST FOUND HIM ON THE GROUND.

SIGH
SHEESH! THAT WAS A MESSED-UP ANTIQUE SHOP!
WHAT A WASTE OF TIME!
EVERY TIME I RUSH SOMETHING IT'S ALWAYS A DISASTER.
AW, MAN! WHAT SHOULD I DO ABOUT SAYAMA'S PRESENT? AM I GONNA HAVE TO BLACKMAIL SOMEBODY FOR CASH OR WHAT?
UH... YAMATO?
SOMETHING WAS WEIRD ABOUT THAT BOY.
SURE, WHEN WE WENT IN I SAID YOUR NAME...
...AND *YOU* SAID ULTIMO, BUT THAT'S NOT EVEN THE WEIRDEST THING.

DID YOU SEE?
FIRST HE WAS ALL BEAT-UP AND DIRTY...
...BUT AFTER HE HUGGED YOU, HE WAS ALL CLEAN AND SHINY...
UM, IT'S JUST YOUR IMAGINATION. THERE WASN'T ANY WOW FACTOR TO THAT GUY AT ALL.
NO, IT WAS MORE THAN A WOW FACTOR!
AND MOST OF ALL...
...HE WAS ONLY A PUPPET WHEN WE WERE LOOKING AT HIM. NO WAY HE WAS A REAL KID.
...
MAYBE.

MAYBE?! WHY--
I DON'T WANT ANY PART OF THIS.
!
ACTUALLY, NOW I DO HAVE THIS OTHER NAME IN MY HEAD TOO.
DUNSTAN!!

AS SOON AS I LOOKED AT HIM...
...I KNEW NOTHING GOOD WAS GOING TO COME OF IT.
I MEAN, I'M NOT REINCARNATED. COME ON. BUT I STILL DON'T WANT ANYTHING TO DO WITH HIM.
AND SAYAMA HAS NOTHING TO DO WITH THIS MESS EITHER.
...
BUT, YAMATO...
...I'M WORRIED...
...BECAUSE I KNOW BETTER THAN ANYONE ELSE HOW, IF SOMETHING HAPPENED, YOU'RE THE TYPE WHO COULDN'T LET IT ALONE.
TOO BAD.
YOU'RE ALREADY INVOLVED...

...
AGARI
YAMATO.

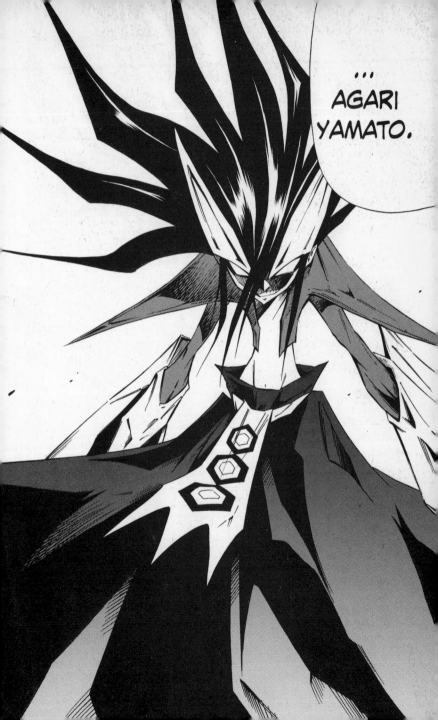

BOOM
YOU WERE LOOKING FOR A GIFT AND FOUND ME.
WHAAAT?!
KARAKURI HENGE!

TURTLE SAW!!

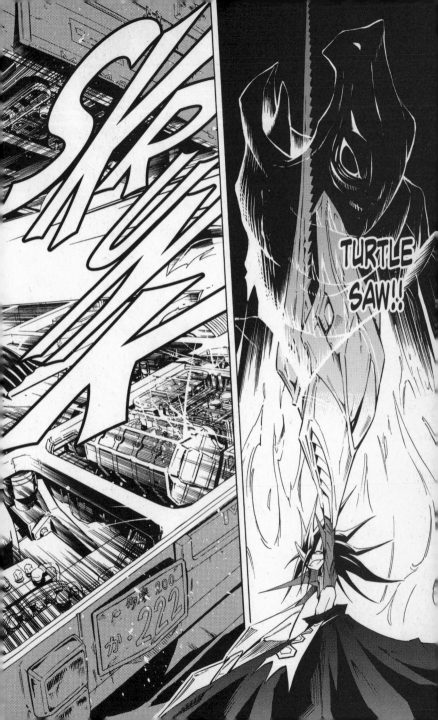

GRIND!!!

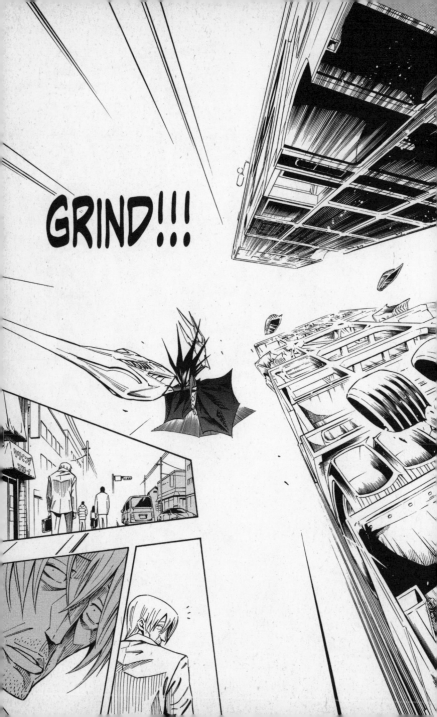

GYAAAAAAAHH!!
HAIR WISH.
スナック 夢
いしかわ精肉

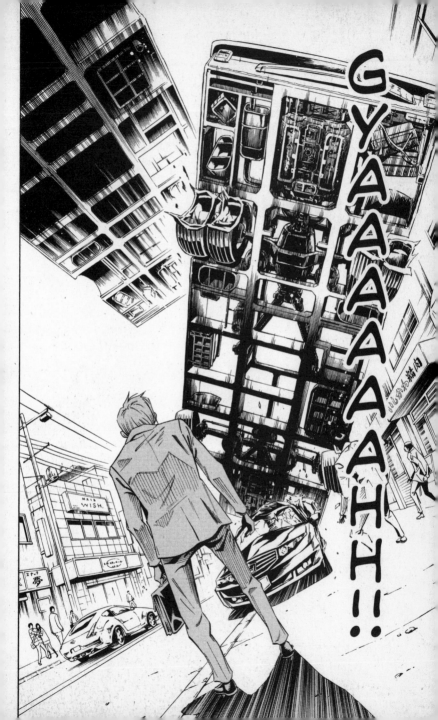

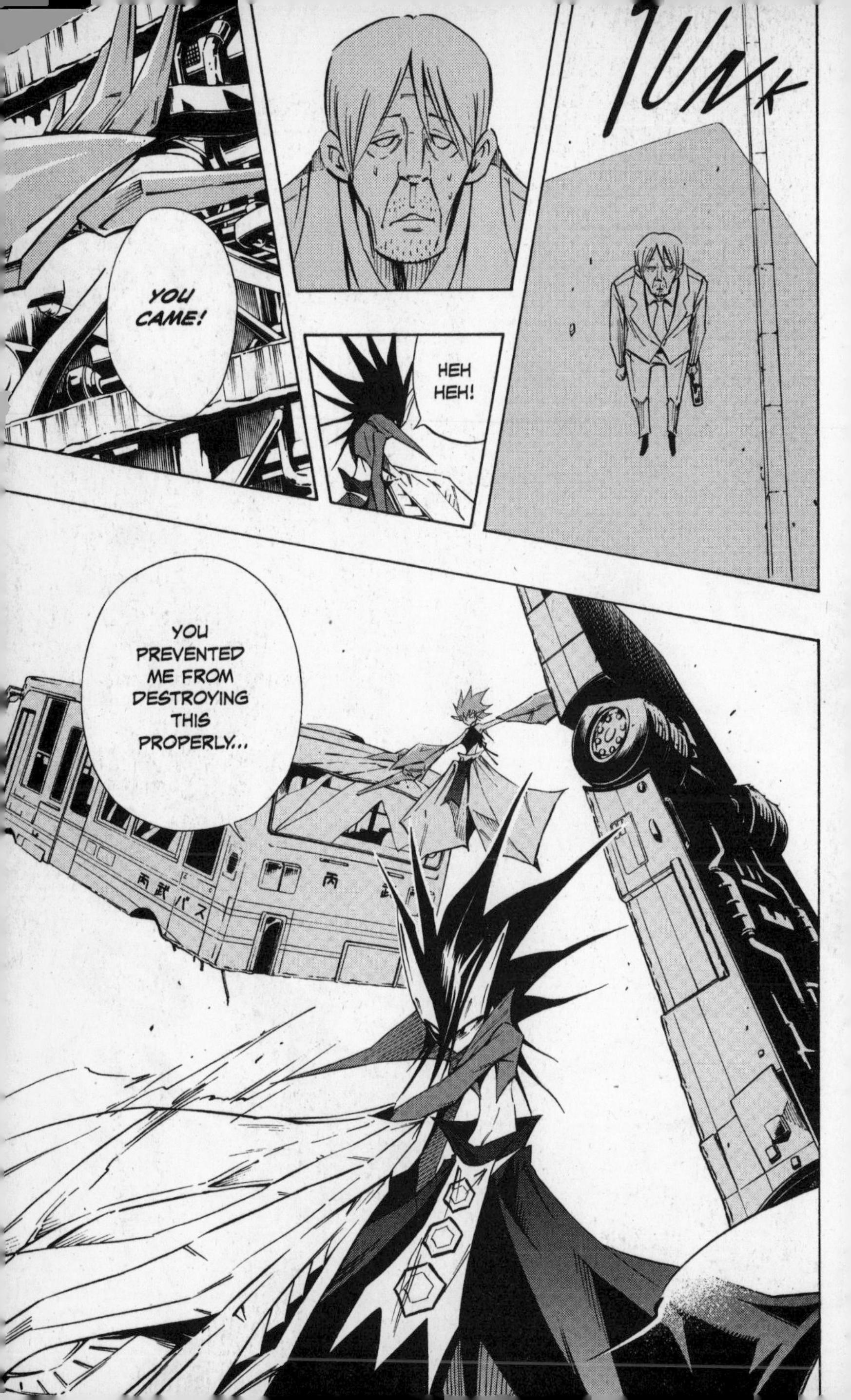
ZUNK
HEH HEH!
YOU CAME!
YOU PREVENTED ME FROM DESTROYING THIS PROPERLY...

...ULTIMO!!!

丙
ULTIMO?!
HUH
YAMATO...
...THE BUS IS FLYING!
SORRY, YAMATO-SAMA. I FOLLOWED YOU.
!
YOU'RE... FLYING...?

GASP
HEY, WHAT'S THAT?!
IS THAT BUS FLYING?
IS THAT PERSON FLYING?
AN ACCIDENT?!
HIS ARMS ARE TOO LONG, RIGHT?
HEH HEH... MANY MORE PEOPLE THAN BEFORE, HUH?
MURMUR
MURMUR
MURMUR
MURMUR
MURMUR
LOOK AT THE ONLOOKERS THAT HAVE GATHERED!
IT COULD BE WELL WORTH MY WHILE TO GO ON A RAMPAGE, DON'T YOU THINK, ULTIMO?
VICE...
...YOU ARE SO FULL OF POWER...
SURELY YOU HAVEN'T--

HUH?
WHAT'S IT GOT TO DO WITH YOU, ULTIMO?
THIS ISN'T GOOD.
HE'S ALREADY FOUND A MASTER.
KLIK
WHICH MEANS HIS MASTER MUST BE NEARBY.
WHO...
...IS HIS MASTER?!
KLIK
LOOKING FOR MY MASTER?
YOU THINK YOU CAN STOP HIM FIRST...
NING
...!
HEH HEH HEH!
OH RIGHT, YOU COULD NEVER DO SOMETHING SO SNEAKY!
222

YOU'RE...
...TOO GOOD FOR THAT.

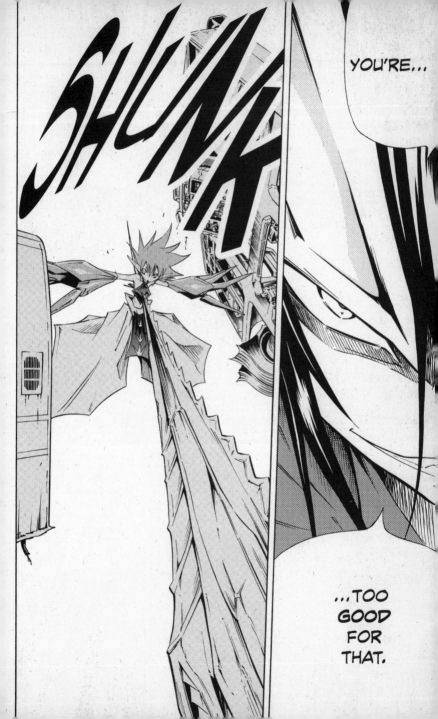

...
SHLUK
UGK...
HEH HEH... FOOL! WITHOUT A MASTER, YOU HARDLY HAVE ANY POWER.
AND WHAT CAN YOU DO WITH BOTH HANDS BUSY TRYING TO PROTECT BYSTANDERS?

IF GOOD FOUGHT EVIL, WHICH WOULD BE STRONGER?
EVIL, OF COURSE.
UNGH...
WHOOPS.
BE CAREFUL HOW YOU MOVE, ULTIMO.
A KARAKURI DÔJI'S SOURCE OF LIFE...
...IS HIS SPIRIT.

MY TURTLE SAW IS DANGEROUSLY CLOSE TO YOUR SPIRIT.
KLAKKLAKKLAK
DID YOU FORGET THAT IF A KARAKURI DÔJI SPIRIT DIES, HE STOPS WORKING?
YAMATO!
HEY!
AAGH!
EEK!
WHAT'S GOING ON?!
...
THIS IS SERIOUS!
WE NEED TO GET OUTTA HERE!

HEH HEH...
WE HAVEN'T KNOWN EACH OTHER LONG, ULTIMO, BUT WHETHER YOU CRY OR LAUGH...
...YOU'RE GOING TO BREAK NOW...
...AND THE WORLD WILL BE *MINE*.
GOOD-BYE...
...ULTIMO.

AGH...
YAMATO-SAMA...

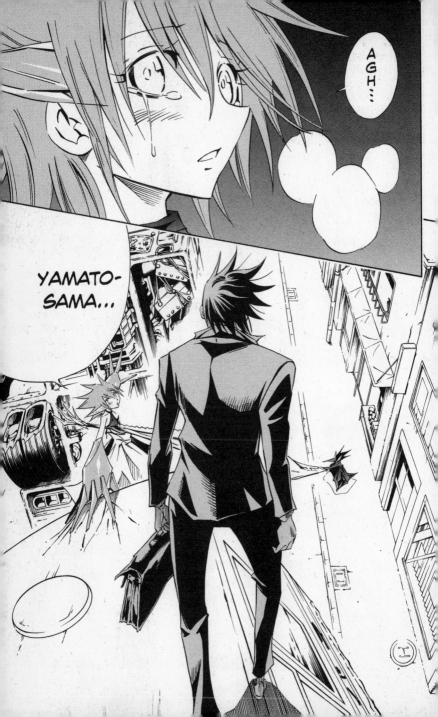

HWOOO
...
SKREEK
SHLUK

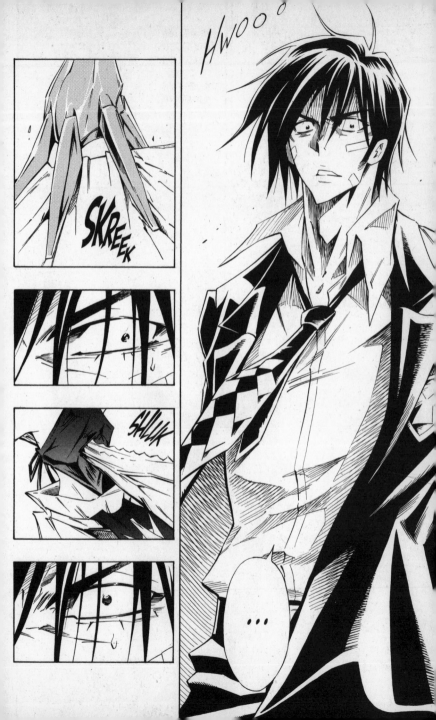

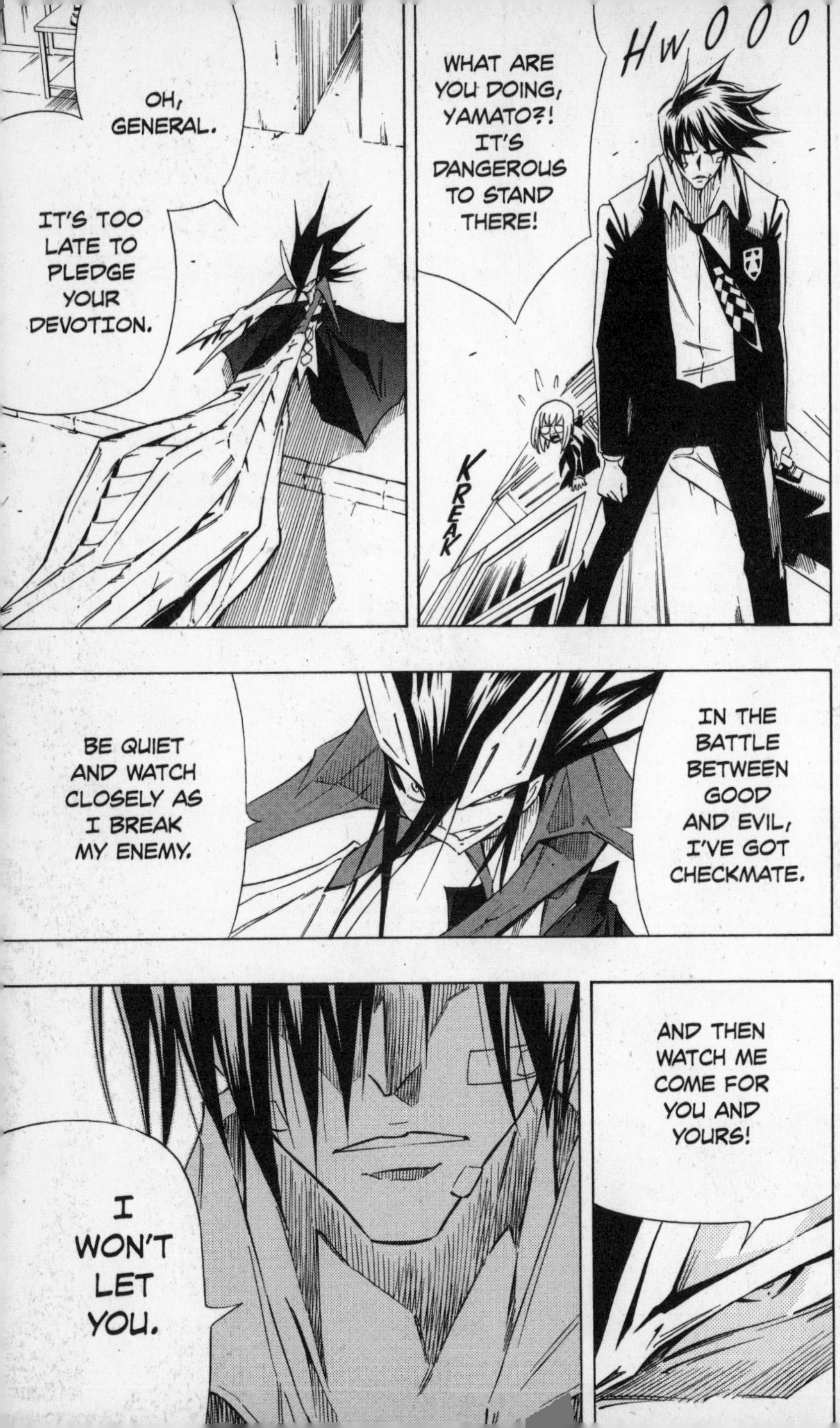
HwOOO
WHAT ARE YOU DOING, YAMATO?! IT'S DANGEROUS TO STAND THERE!
KREAK
OH, GENERAL.
IT'S TOO LATE TO PLEDGE YOUR DEVOTION.
IN THE BATTLE BETWEEN GOOD AND EVIL, I'VE GOT CHECKMATE.
BE QUIET AND WATCH CLOSELY AS I BREAK MY ENEMY.
AND THEN WATCH ME COME FOR YOU AND YOURS!
I WON'T LET YOU.

WHOOSH
I WON'T LET YOU HURT SAYAMA! I'M GOING TO DESTROY YOU!!!

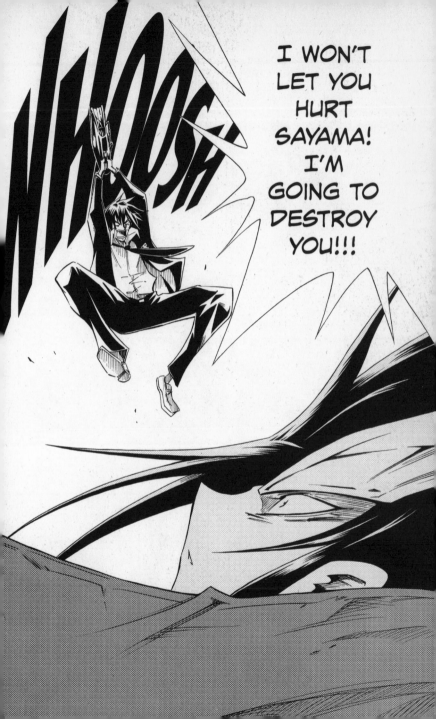

SAYAMA?!
DESTROY? YOU? ME? WITH THAT BAG?
HE'S JUST AS SCATTERED AS EVER.
NO MATTER HOW YOU LOOK AT IT...
...IT'S TIME TO DIE, YAMATO AGARI.
YES...
YOU'LL DO ANYTHING TO PROTECT WHAT'S IMPORTANT TO YOU.
YOU TAKE ULTI FOR SOMEONE'S CHILD. AND YOUR ATTITUDE TOWARD VICE. EVERYTHING YOU DO IS JUST LIKE IT USED TO BE.

THAT ALONE MAKES ULTI HAPPY, AND GIVES HIM STRENGTH.
YOU'VE DIVERTED VICE'S ATTENTION FOR A MOMENT.
I WILL DRAW FORTH MY REMAINING STRENGTH TO STRIKE AT HIM.

EVEN IF IT COSTS ME MY LIFE, I WILL STOP HIM!
KARAKURI HENGE!
CRANE SWORD!!

MILLENNIUM
CUT!!

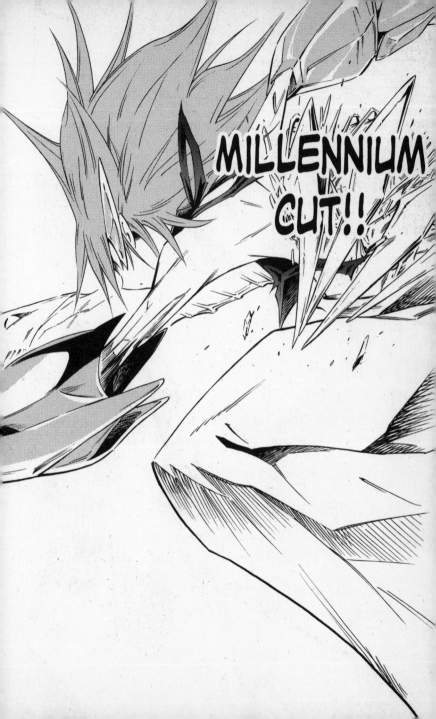

DO YOU SEE, VICE?
WHEN TROUBLE STRIKES, GOOD WILL ALWAYS HAVE FRIENDS. EVIL HAS NO ONE.
GOODBYE, YAMATO-SAMA...

KARAKURIDÔJI
ULTIMO

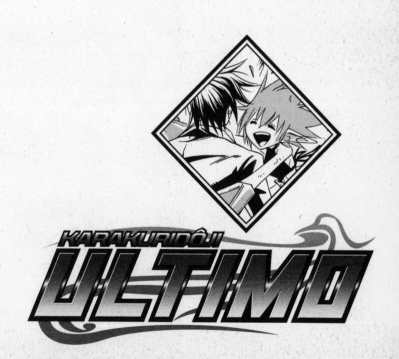

ACT 3
A BLAZE SURROUNDS YAMATO

KARAKURIDÔJI
ULTIMO

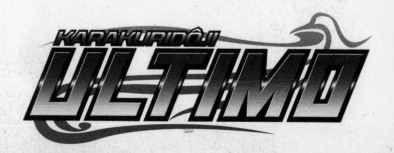

KREAK

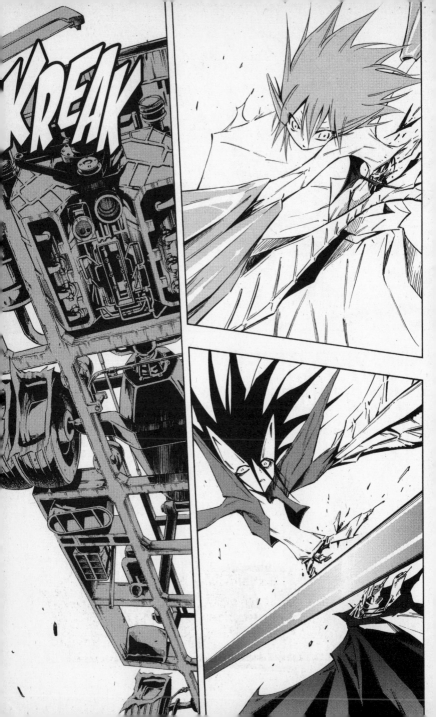

WHOA!
CHATTER
AN EXPLOSION ?!
TERRORISTS!
田茄子駅
FWOOSH
...
EEK
AAGH

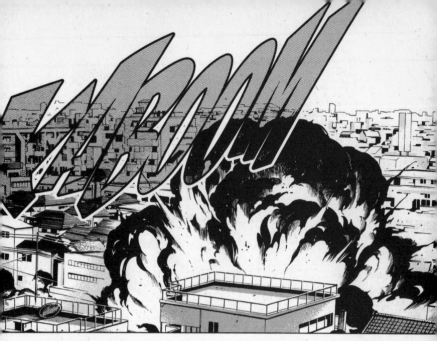

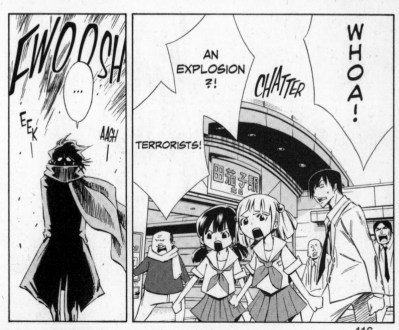

LIVIM LIVIM
FWOOSH
FWOOSH

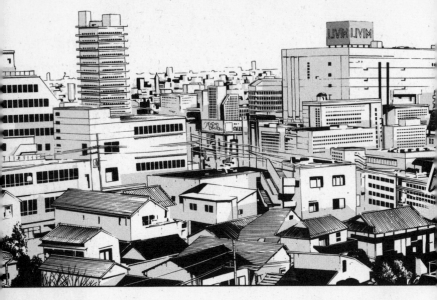

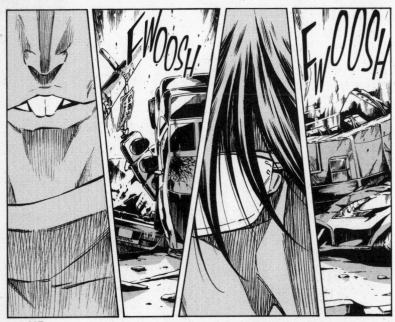

THIS IS CRAZY.
K (31) Unemployed

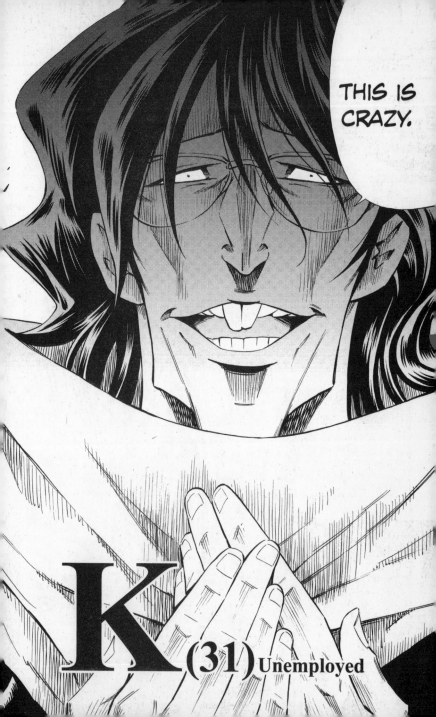

NNGH...
GASP
YAMATO!
ARE YOU OKAY, YAMATO?! HANG ON!
UGH... RUNE? YOU ALL RIGHT?
YEAH!
AAGH
THAT ULTIMO BOY SAVED EVERYONE!
EEK
NO ONE'S HURT!
ULTIMO?!

ULTIMO!

!

HUHH?

...

HEY! YOU OKAY?!

HEY!!!

YAMATO!

OH NO!

SHOOSH

ULTIMO ...?
WEIRD...
HE'S LIKE A PUPPET AGAIN. HE CAN'T MOVE.
AND HE LOOKS BROKEN.

SO HE'S REALLY JUST...
TAK
A KARAKURI DÔJI!
!

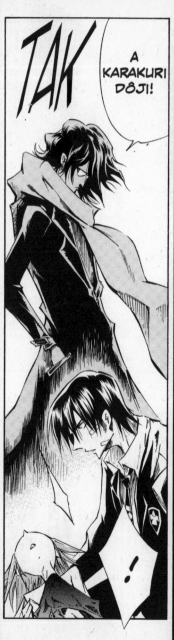

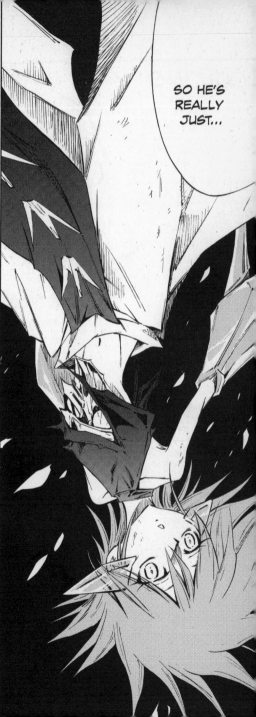

HIS SPIRIT SPHERE IS BROKEN.
ONCE THAT HAPPENS, THERE'S LITTLE HOPE OF RECOVERY.
DON'T EXPECT MUCH.
HUH?
WHO ARE YOU?
K.
I ENCOUNTERED THE KARAKURI DÔJI EXACTLY ONE YEAR AGO IN THIS VERY TOWN.
...
I FOUND ONE ON THE VERGE OF DEATH. AND I FIXED HIM.
HIS NAME'S WRITTEN ON HIS COAT...

YOU MAY CALL ME THE VICE MASTER.
WHUMP

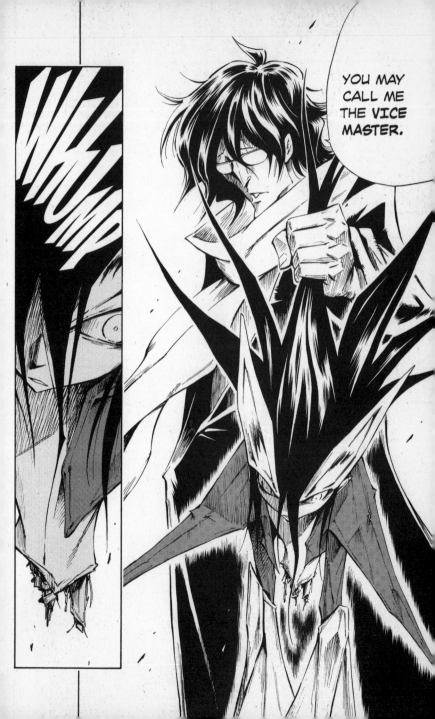

VICE MASTER?!
YOU KNOW THESE TWO?!
NOT VERY BRIGHT, ARE YOU?
AFTER ALL I'VE DONE, HOW COULD I *NOT* KNOW THEM?
HUH?!
URGH
THIS JERK...
I DON'T NEED TO TELL YOU ANY MORE THAN THAT.
AFTER I WENT TO ALL THE TROUBLE OF FIXING IT, YOU RUINED IT AGAIN.
WITH VICE IN MY POWER, I NEVER WOULD HAVE HAD TO WORK AGAIN!
NOTHING COULD STOP ME!
I QUIT MY JOB AND RENTED A ROOM.

WE EXCHANGED THE PLEDGE OF DEVOTION!
GRR
BUT YOU...
GRR
GRR
GRR
...BROKE, YOU STUPID DOLL!
WHACK

HUH?!
WHAT ARE YOU GONNA DO ABOUT MY JOB, MY RENT?!
GIVE IT BACK! THAT'S 84,000 YEN FOR 12 MONTHS!!!
YOU MADE ALL THIS MESS!
WHAT IF I GOT ARRESTED?
WHAT WOULD MY GRANDMA THINK?!!!
WHAT IS WITH THIS GUY?
FIRST HE'S CREEPY, THEN HE THROWS A FIT...
HEY.
CHAK
!
GAAAAAH!!!

KNOCK IT OFF, CREEP!!!
UNH!!!

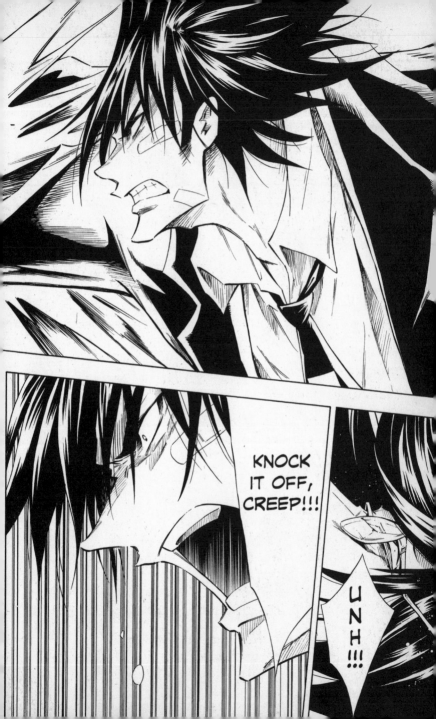

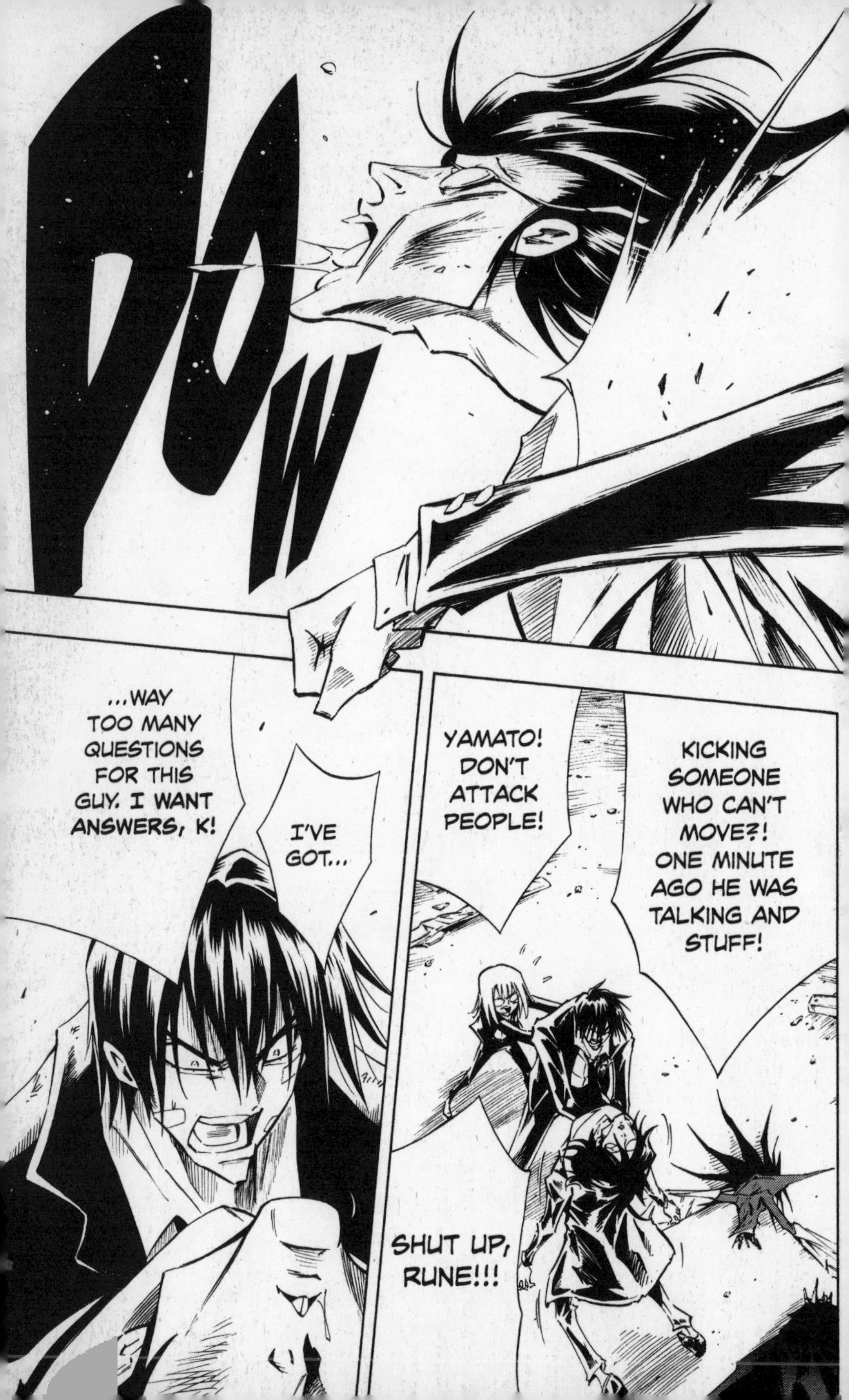
POW
KICKING SOMEONE WHO CAN'T MOVE?! ONE MINUTE AGO HE WAS TALKING AND STUFF!
YAMATO! DON'T ATTACK PEOPLE!
SHUT UP, RUNE!!!
I'VE GOT...
...WAY TOO MANY QUESTIONS FOR THIS GUY. I WANT ANSWERS, K!

YOU'RE PASSING OUT?!!
ARE YOU THAT WEAK?!
WEEOO
!
YOU!!!
WHAT ARE YOU DOING HERE?
YOU KIDS DID ALL THIS?! NO WAY!

IF YOU REALLY DID ALL THIS, I, POLICE INSPECTOR DARUMADA OF THE TANASU POLICE DEPARTMENT...
...WILL NOT LET YOU OFF EASY!!!
BAM
警部
Police Inspector
達磨田正美
Darumada Masami
POLICE
警視庁
Darumada Masami (44)
Heh heh heh! Hey, Boss...
HUH?
ANOTHER FACE I KNOW!!!
SHUT UP! I'VE GOT ENOUGH TO WORRY ABOUT WITHOUT YOU STARTING IN!

WAAAH! WHAT DO WE DO, YAMATO? THE POLICE ARE HERE!
GASP
BUT THIS IS GOOD.
IF WE TALK TO THEM, WE CAN CLEAR UP EVERYTHING, ALL THIS MECHANICAL BOY BUSINESS.
NNK...
HELP ME, INSPECTOR. THIS GUY BLEW UP THE BUS.
I TRIED TO CATCH HIM, BUT HE BEAT ME UP AND TOOK ME HOSTAGE...
NNGH...
...GGHH...

WHAAAAT?!!
HEY! LIAR!
DON'T MOVE!!!
WHOOSH
WE'LL TALK OVER THE DETAILS AT THE STATION.
I'M ARRESTING YOU FOR ASSAULT AND BATTERY.
VSHK

HOW?!
A gun?
!
HEH HEH HEH!
SERVES YOU RIGHT, AGARI YAMATO.
I CAN'T...
...UNDERSTAND WHY THAT SWEET LITTLE KARAKURI DÔJI, FULL OF GOODNESS, WOULD TAKE SOMEONE AS VIOLENT AS YOU FOR A MASTER.
?!
BUT...
...WHO IS THIS SAYAMA YOU WERE YELLING ABOUT? YOUR GIRLFRIEND?
HUH?! SHE'S GOT NOTHING TO DO WITH YOU!
WHUF
WHUF
HEH HEH!
WHUF
SHE CAN'T BE YOUR GIRLFRIEND...
...BUT I BET SHE'S CUTE.
WHUF
I'M JEALOUS.

I'D LIKE TO MEET HER.
WHILE YOU'RE IN CONFINEMENT. ♡
HUF
HUFF
HUFFF
YOU JERK!!!
TCH!
KSHAK
HEH
HOW LONG ARE YOU GOING TO SLEEP, VICE?

PROTECT ME.
GAH!
SPLAT
BLOOD!
THE MECHANICAL BOY'S HAND!!!
GAH! WHAT'S THAT?!!

UNTIL HE FULFILLS HIS FINAL ROLE, A KARAKURI DÔJI MUST OBEY HIS MASTER.
HE MUST PROTECT HIS MASTER AND FULFILL HIS MASTER'S WISHES.
KLAK
KLAK
KLAK
IT MAY TAKE SOME TIME TO REPAIR HIM...
...BUT MY GAME HAS JUST BEGUN.
KLAK
KLAK
KLAK
KLAK
KLAK
KLAK
KLAK
KLAK

'TIL WE MEET AGAIN!
WHOOSH
THOUGH I'D REALLY RATHER WE DIDN'T.
HE FLEW AWAY!
A MONSTER!
...
...
(SENJO ACADEMY)
占城高等学校
AND THEN GUESS WHAT!

THE BUS GOT BASHED IN TWO!
HE WAS FLYING! AND HIS ARMS WERE REEEALLY LONG!
IT WAS...
...AWE-SOME!!!
Oume Hibari (16)

...
Matsumoto Kiyose (17)
Otake Akitsu (16)
UM, I NEED A FAVOR, UME. CAN YOU TRY TO TALK A LITTLE LESS CRAZY? NO ONE UNDERSTANDS YOU.
SORRY...
HEY, WHAT'S THAT MEEEAAN?
GOOD MORNING, EVERYONE!
RATTLE

?
WAIT, WHAT'S THE MATTER?
Sayama Makoto (17)
OH, GOOD MORNING, SAYAMA. UME SAYS A BUS BLEW UP IN FRONT OF THE STATION THIS MORNING.
BUS BLEW WHAT?
2-B
NO!
AND WHAT'S MORE...
...YAMATO AND RUNE WERE THERE!!!

HUH?
WHAD-DAYA MEAN, HUH?
WHAT DON'T YOU GET?
一、機敏に行動
二、授業の始ま
AH HA HA! OH, NOTHING! IT WAS NOTHING!
ANYWAY, ISN'T TODAY SAYAMA'S BIRTHDAY?
OH, RIGHT! EVERYONE'S GOING TO THE PARTY, RIGHT?
BUT...
...I SAW YAMATO COMING TO SCHOOL LIKE NORMAL.
I HOPE HE'S ALL RIGHT.

HUFF
HUFF
HUFF
GOOD, RIGHT? NO ONE WILL FIND US HERE.
WHEN VICE MORPHED, WE TOOK OUR CHANCE AND GOT AWAY!
HA HA HA HA HA
IT'S NOT GOOD AT ALL!!!
YAMATO, THIS IS SERIOUS!
WE SHOULD HAVE GONE WITH THE POLICE!
NOW IT'S EVEN WORSE!
AND WE EVEN BROUGHT THAT BOY!
LPG

WE COULDN'T JUST LEAVE HIM.
!
HE TRIED TO HELP US.
THAT COP LOOKED DIRTY. YOU WANT HIM TO HAVE ULTIMO?
SO WHAT?
WHAT ARE YOU GONNA DO?!!!
I'M GOING...
...TO FIX HIM.

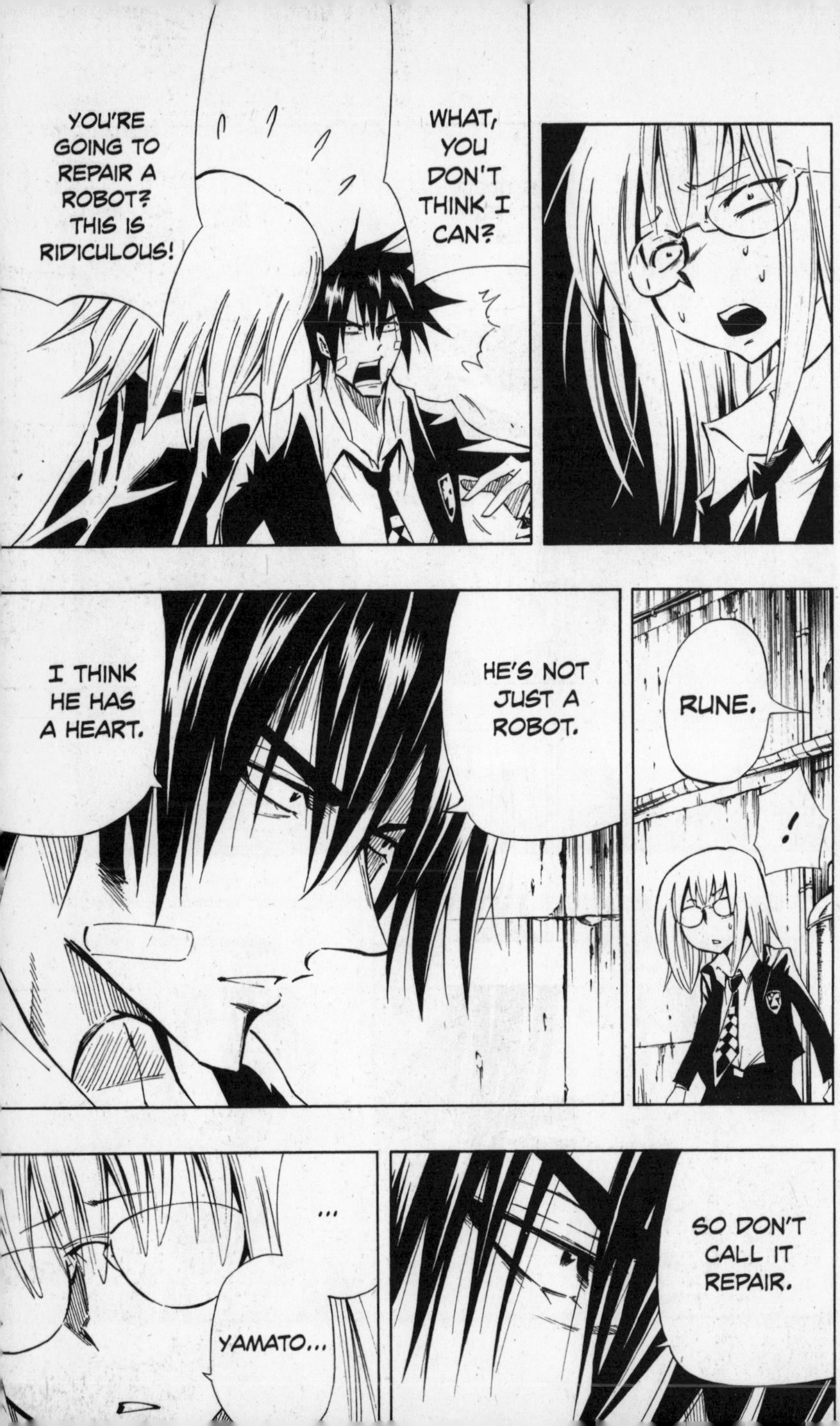
YOU'RE GOING TO REPAIR A ROBOT? THIS IS RIDICULOUS!
WHAT, YOU DON'T THINK I CAN?
RUNE.
HE'S NOT JUST A ROBOT.
I THINK HE HAS A HEART.
SO DON'T CALL IT REPAIR.
...
YAMATO...

...YOU'RE RIGHT.

I MEAN, YOU'RE PROBABLY RIGHT. IT MIGHT BE TRUE.

...GOT TO GO TO SCHOOL.

I'VE...

I DON'T WANT TO GET INVOLVED EITHER. BUT I THINK I'M ALREADY IN TOO DEEP TO GET AWAY FROM IT NOW.

I'M SORRY, RUNE!

...SIMPLY BY PRETENDING TO FORGET ABOUT THAT OLD GUY DUNSTAN, THAT DIRTY COP, K AND-- MOST OF ALL-- THE MECHANICAL BOYS... THE... THE KARAKURI DÔJI!
THIS WON'T END...
THE FIRST THING TO DO IS FIX ULTIMO.
AND I HAVE AN IDEA HOW TO DO THAT.

I WON'T LET HIM LAY A FINGER ON SAYAMA!!!

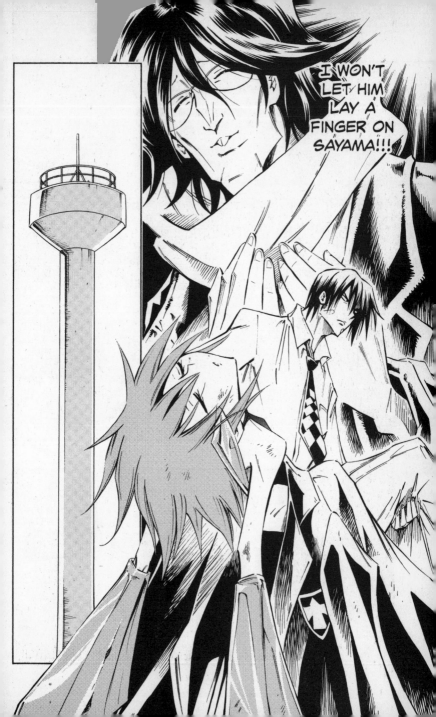

I GOT HOME BY THE BACK ROADS.

ALL RIGHT.

47

NOW I JUST HAVE TO MAKE IT TO MY ROOM WITHOUT LETTING ANYONE SEE ME.

RUSTLE

I DON'T THINK ANYTHING WILL HAPPEN, BUT I GOTTA BE SUPER CAREFUL!

HEH HEH HEH

YAMATO?

GASP! MOM!!!
Agari Fushimi (32)
WHY AREN'T YOU AT SCHOOL?
Wait, you're not... going number two out here are you?!
NO... OF COURSE NOT, I'M...
CAN YOU JUST GET THROUGH GRADUATION?

PROBABLY.
IF I DON'T GET ARRESTED...
FINE.
I'VE ALWAYS TAKEN CARE OF YOU... AND BY MYSELF I MIGHT ADD. SO THE VERY LEAST YOU CAN DO IS NOT WASTE WHAT I'VE PAID TO YOUR SCHOOL.
I'LL BE LATE AGAIN TONIGHT, SO EAT WHATEVER YOU LIKE FOR DINNER.
AND...
...DON'T BRING YOUR WEIRD FRIENDS INTO YOUR ROOM.
And don't go number two outside...
SURE...
WHEW, I GOT LUCKY!
Well, yeah, about that number two thing...
47-402
東 AGARI
THAT WAS CLOSE! I DIDN'T EXPECT TO BUMP INTO MOM!
IF SHE'D BEEN IN A BAD MOOD, SHE'D HAVE KICKED MY BUTT!

OKAY, I'M IN MY ROOM.
SO, ULTI...
ULTIMO...
UH-OH, THESE INJURIES ARE REALLY BAD.
BUT WHEN WE WERE OUT IN THE DARK ALLEYS, I COULD SEE HIS SPIRIT SPHERE SHINING FAINTLY.
SO HE'S NOT DEAD.

DID YOU SEE?
FIRST HE WAS ALL BEAT-UP AND DIRTY...
...BUT AFTER HE HUGGED YOU, HE WAS ALL CLEAN AND SHINY...
ULTI WOKE UP BECAUSE YOU CAME WITHIN HIS RANGE.
ONCE THAT HAPPENS, THERE'S LITTLE HOPE OF RECOVERY.
DON'T EXPECT MUCH.
WHICH MEANS...
...ONCE I DO SOME SPECIFIC THING, YOU WILL RECOVER ON YOUR OWN.

THE
ONLY
THING
TO
DO...

...IS RENEW THE PLEDGE OF DEVOTION.
BUT WHAT IS THAT? WHAT'S IT MEAN? WHAT DO I DO?!!
GULP

...WAIT, IS THAT REALLY WHAT I'M SUPPOSED TO DO?

YOU WAKE UP A SLEEPING PRINCESS...

...HOW DO I MAKE THIS WORK?

UNH...

A KISS SEEMS CRAZY... BUT WHATEVER, I DON'T HAVE TIME TO THINK OF ANYTHING ELSE!!!

FWIK

WAP

I'M SORRY, SAYAMA!!!

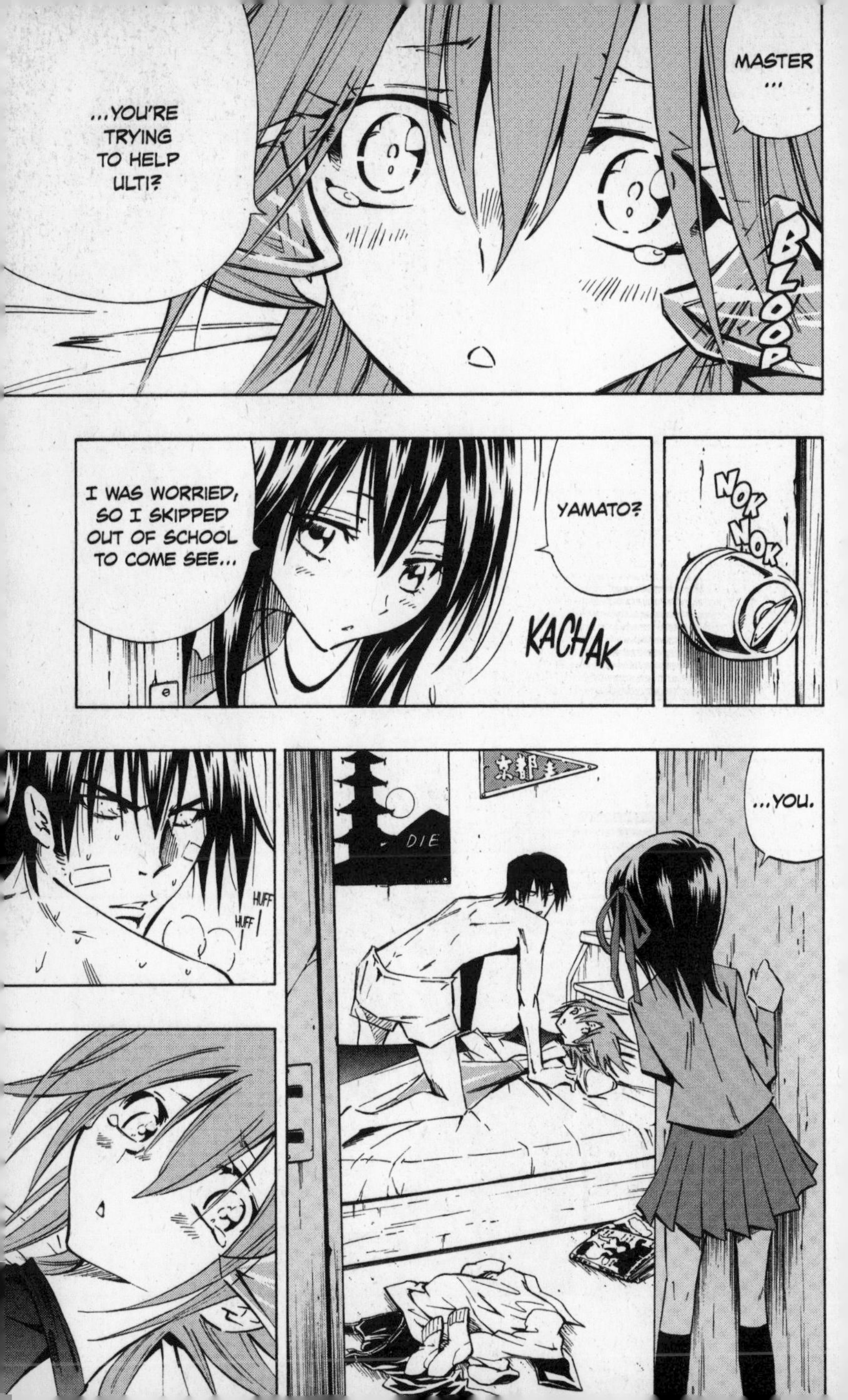
MASTER...
...YOU'RE TRYING TO HELP ULTI?
BLOOP
NOK NOK
KACHAK
YAMATO?
I WAS WORRIED, SO I SKIPPED OUT OF SCHOOL TO COME SEE...
...YOU.
DIE
HUFF HUFF

HEH...

THUD—

AGH!

SAYAMA...

KLIK

MASTER!
BE STRONG, YAMATO-SAMA!
HA HA HA HA
OH...
ENVY!
KLAK

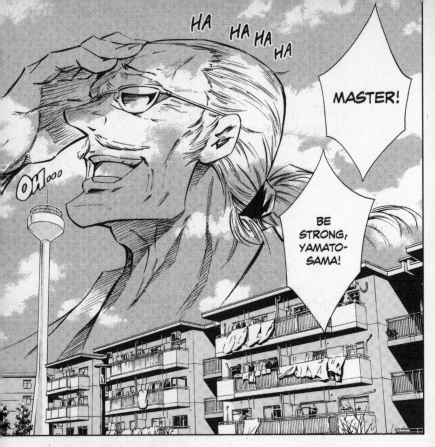

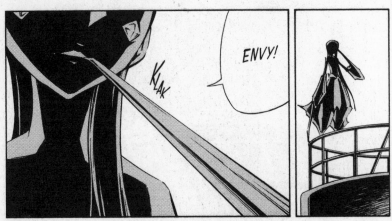

OH...

KARAKURIDÔJI
ULTIMO

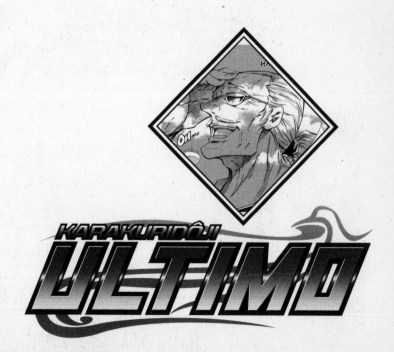

...THE TIME HAS COME TO TOPPLE THE NOBILITY!

TONIGHT WE TAKE THE CAPITAL BY STORM.

ACT 4: A DREAM OF RASEIMON

ARE YOU...

...READY?

Yamato (19): Bandit

YAAAAAAHHHHH!!!

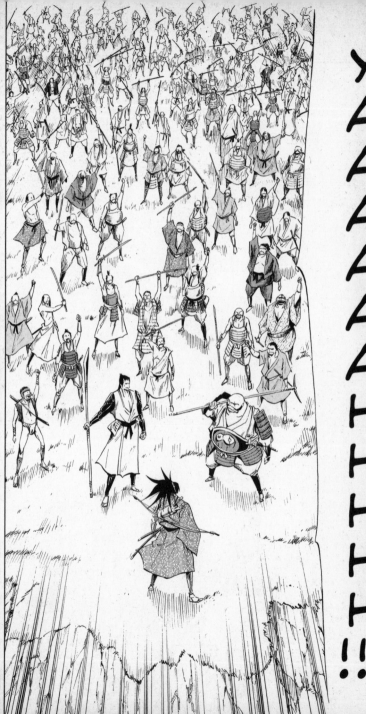

ACT 4
A DREAM OF RASEIMON

HA HA! CHIEF BOSS DID GOOD.
YAAH
YEAH. IN THREE YEARS...
YAAAH
...OUR SMALL BAND HAS GROWN TO AN ARMY!
AS THE NOBILITY GROWS MORE CORRUPT...
...MORE PEOPLE OPPOSE THEM.
AND NOW...
...WE HAVE *HIM.*

THAT OLD MAN LEFT US SOMETHING INCREDIBLE.

ULTIMO.

TODAY IS THE BATTLE, CORRECT?

SORRY, ULTI. I WASN'T CALLING YOU.

MASTER!

IT IS.

HA HA HA! YOU'RE JOINED AT THE HIP!

BUT MANY WILL DIE TODAY.

I WOULD UNDERSTAND IF TODAY YOU WISHED TO LEAVE.

YOU HAVE BEEN LOYAL.

DISTINGUISHING BETWEEN GOOD AND EVIL IS NOT SO SIMPLE TO DETERMINE.

THUS, THE KARAKURI DÔJI MUST SERVE UNDER MASTERS.

FWUMP

!

UNTIL I LEARN...
...PLEASE KEEP ULTI BY YOUR SIDE, YAMATO-SAMA.
ULTI...
FWSH
FWSH
FWSH

KLOP

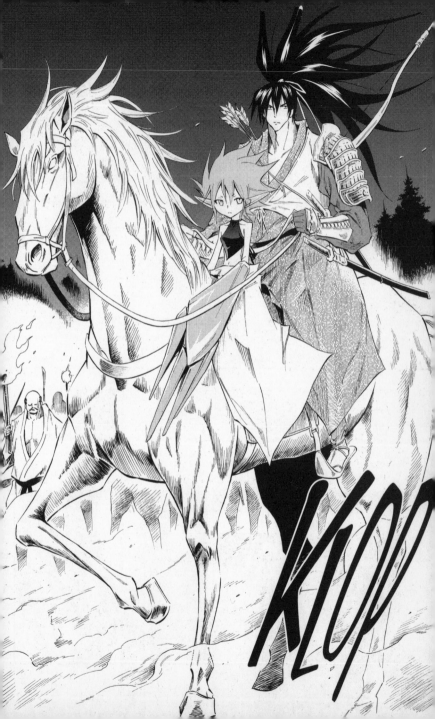

RASEIMON GATE.
THE PALACES OF THE NOBILITY LIE BEYOND.
WHAT A WRECK.
IT'S ABANDONED AND ROTTING. VICTIMS OF PLAGUE LIE EVERYWHERE.
羅世門
ONCE THIS WAS THE CAPITAL'S GLORIOUS MAIN GATE.
HOWEVER DESOLATE THE LAND IS, DON'T DROP YOUR GUARD.
ULTI AND I WILL BREAK THROUGH.

WE'LL SHOW YOU...
...A NEW STYLE OF COMBO FIGHT THAT WAS THREE YEARS IN THE MAKING!
KLOP
CHARGE!!!
GRAAAAAH!!!

THAT'S FAR ENOUGH.
I ENVY YOU.
YOU MAY NOT PASS THIS GATE.
SHING
!!!
KLAK KLAK
KARAKURI HENGE!
!

KUMO KIRIMARU!
SPIDER SLAYER!!
WHAM
WHAT?!
HOW?!

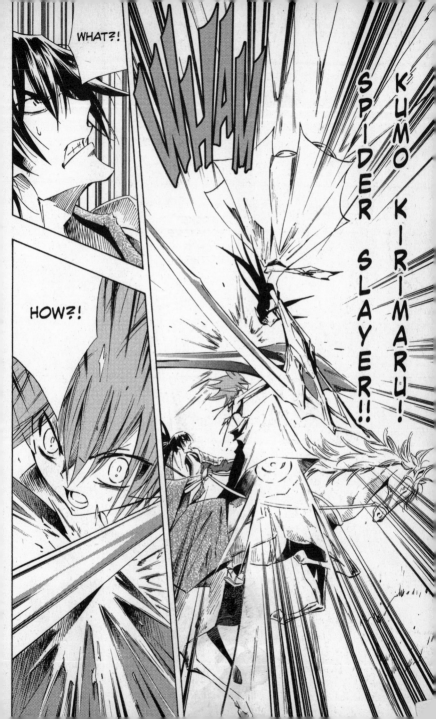

ULTIMATE GOOD AND ULTIMATE EVIL!
I THOUGHT VICE AND ULTI WERE THE ONLY TWO!
BUT HE HAS TRANS-FORMING BLUE GAUNTLETS...
...ROCKET BOOSTERS HIDDEN IN HIS CLOTHES...
...AND KARAKURI DÔJI PINK VISORS!!!
WHOOSH

TUMP
HE'S A KARAKURI DÔJI!!!
THERE IS ANOTHER?!!
!
ULTIMATE ...
...AND PERFECT CANNOT COEXIST.
FOR ONE THING TO FLOURISH, ANOTHER MUST SUFFER.
SHFF

THIS BOY, WHO IS AKIN TO EVIL, COMPENSATES FOR THAT.
HE IS *JEALOUSY*.
DUNSTAN'S NEWEST CREATION BELONGS TO ME!
DADUM

MURMURMURMURMUR
NEWEST CREATION?!
NOBLES HAVE A KARAKURI DÔJI?!
A NOBLE!
DON'T RECOGNIZE HIM!
CHATTER
MUTTER
MUMBLE
WHO IS THAT?!
A NOBLE?!
MUTTER
MUMBLE
MUTTER
MUMBLE
CHATTER
HEY!
BE CALM!
IF I WERE YOU I'D RETREAT RATHER THAN CALM DOWN.
YOU SEEM TO HAVE NO IDEA HOW TO USE A KARAKURI DÔJI!
!

A DÔJI IS STRONGEST WHEN CLOSE TO HIS MASTER, BUT ALSO MORE DANGEROUS.
THE DÔJI MUST THEN HOLD BACK. AND YOU LOOK RIDICULOUS JOINED AT THE HIP, BY THE WAY.
WHAT?!
YOU'RE ARROGANT FOR SOME-ONE SO STUPID!
JEALOUSY.
WITH UNCOMMON SKILL AND UNCEASING EXPERIMENTATION, DR. DUNSTAN HAS CREATED...
TUMP
...SEVERAL NEW DÔJI AND DISTRIBUTED THEM THROUGH-OUT TIME.
!
BEFORE WE EVEN FIGHT, YOU ARE ALREADY OBSOLETE...
...MY *BROTHER*.

WHOOSH
ULTI...!
SEE?
YOUR MOVEMENT IS SLOW, SO YOUR PRECIOUS MASTER WAS OPEN TO ATTACK.
URGH...!
!
AGH!

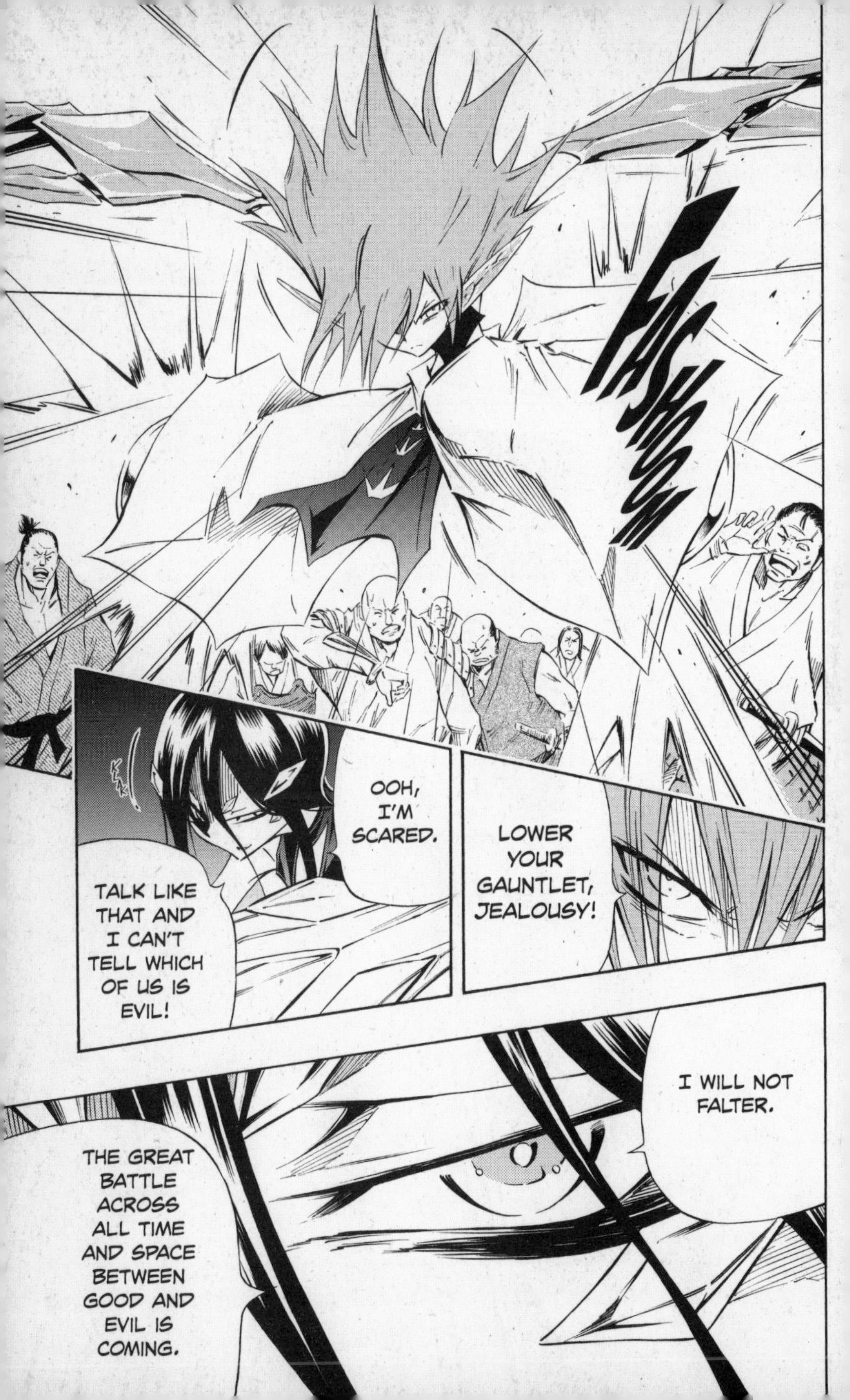
FASHOOM
LOWER YOUR GAUNTLET, JEALOUSY!
OOH, I'M SCARED.
KLAK
TALK LIKE THAT AND I CAN'T TELL WHICH OF US IS EVIL!
I WILL NOT FALTER.
THE GREAT BATTLE ACROSS ALL TIME AND SPACE BETWEEN GOOD AND EVIL IS COMING.

THE HUNDRED MACHINE FUNERAL.

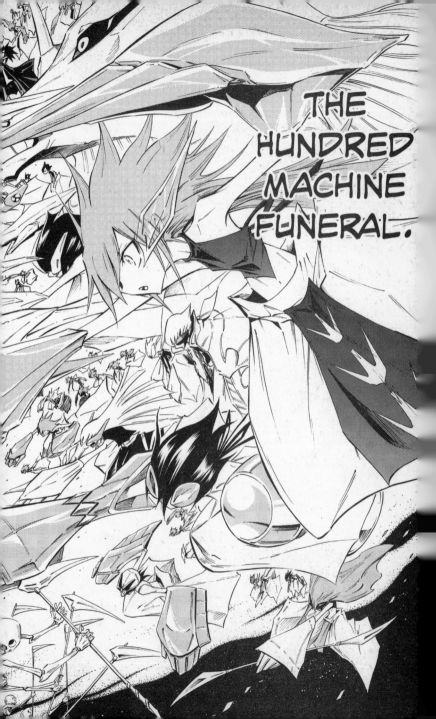

ONE HUNDRED DÔJI IN EVERY FORM IMAGINABLE IN BATTLE!

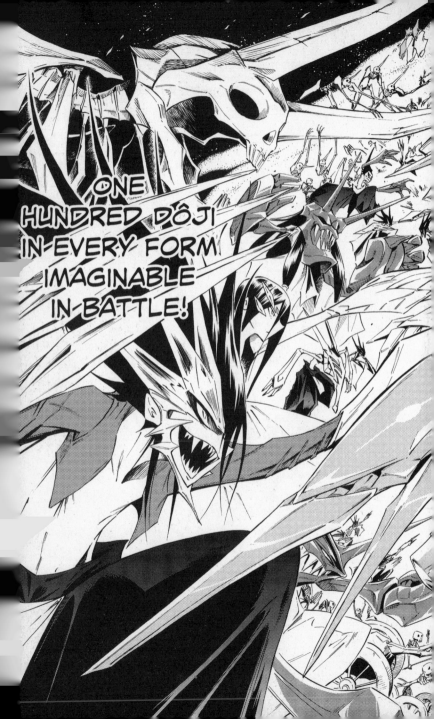

HUNDRED MACHINE FUNERAL?!
DID YOU THINK THE DÔJI SERVE ONLY YOU?
THEY FIGHT ONLY TO PROVE WHICH IS STRONGER, GOOD OR EVIL.
SO OF COURSE, I, YOUR OPPONENT, ALSO HAVE A DÔJI.
OTHERWISE THE FIGHT WOULD NOT BE FAIR.
ARGH!
THAT OLD MAN WAS PLANNING THIS ALL ALONG!
DÔJI SERVE THEIR MASTERS ONLY A SHORT TIME...
...BUT I WILL MAKE FULL USE OF MINE.

AN UNKNOWN NOBLE OF LOW RANK WILL STAND ALONE AGAINST THE BANDITS. AND HE WILL DEFEAT THEM.
!
AND THAT LEGEND WILL PROPEL ME INTO THE RULING CLASS.
YOU ARE...
...UNSCRUPULOUS.
MAYBE. BUT THE PEOPLE...
...WILL CALL ME GOOD.
Iruma Tomomitsu (48)
Unscrupulous noble

ALL RIGHT, JEALOUSY...
...LET US SHOW THE TRUE WAY A MASTER AND HIS DÔJI FIGHT!
KARAKURI HENGE!

TSUCHIGUMO! GROUND SPIDER!!

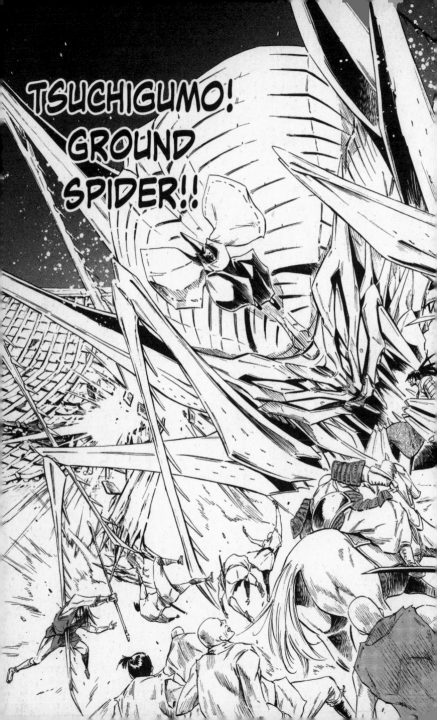

GRAWWWR!
ALL RIGHT THEN, LET'S FIGHT !!!
HMMM...

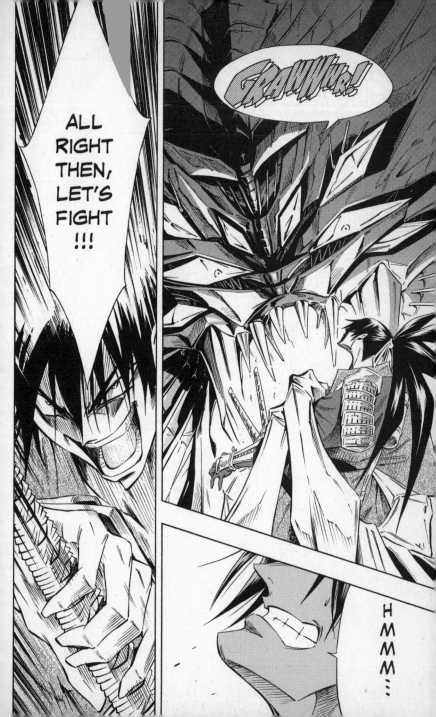

HUH ?!

DIE

DIE

A DREAM?

...

THEY DO!

KARAKURI DŌJI DON'T EXIST...

HA HA... OF COURSE IT WAS...

WHOOSH

THAT MUST MEAN SAYAMA REALLY DID--

...AND IT WASN'T!!!

IT WAS A DREAM...

!!!

SAYAMA...

From Sayama

Soooo

BADUMP BADUMP

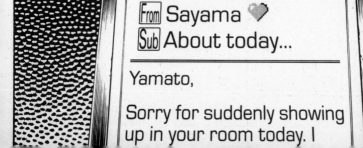

From Sayama 🩵
Sub About today...

Yamato,

Sorry for suddenly showing up in your room today. I

Yamato,

Sorry for suddenly showing up in your room today. I knocked several times, but you didn't answer, so I opened the door.

It looked like you were going to kiss that puppet doll thing...?

I won't tell anyone about this, but it'd probably be best if you don't come to the party tonight.

SPSSHH
TSSSSHH
IT'S OVER.
MY LIFE...
...IS OVER!!!

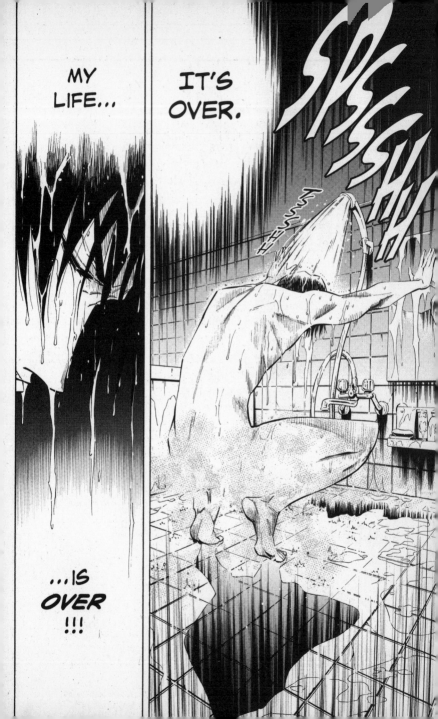

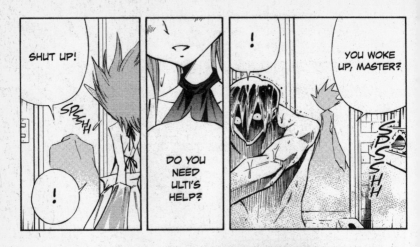

YOU WOKE UP, MASTER?
SPSSHH
!
DO YOU NEED ULTI'S HELP?
SHUT UP!
SPSSHH
!
YOU'VE RUINED MY LIFE!
YOU'RE NOT HURT ANYMORE, RIGHT?
SO YOU CAN LEAVE!
I DON'T WANT YOU HERE ANYMORE!

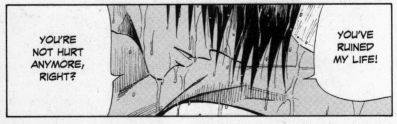

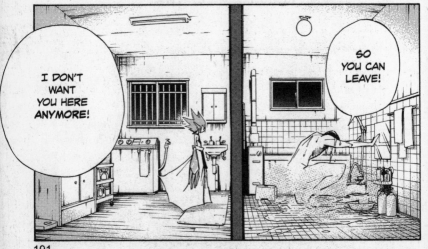

BLOOP
MASTER...
KRASSCHH
ULTIMO IS SORRY, YAMATO-SAMA!!
HWOOO
THE WINDOW...
ACHOO

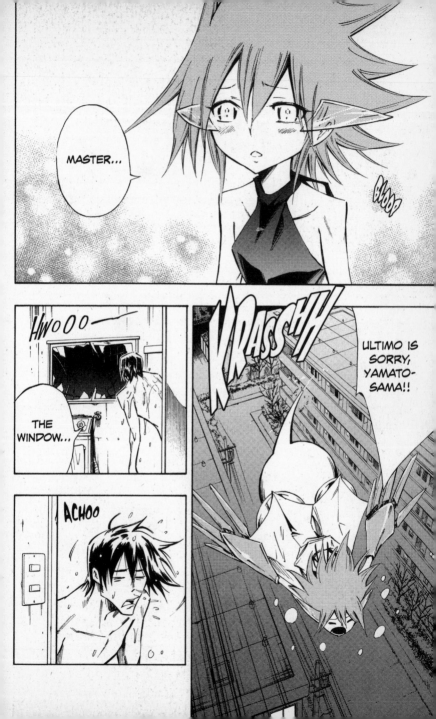

小平
KODAIRA
TAK
TAK
TAK
TAK
TAK
TAK
TAK
TAK TAK TAK TAK TAK

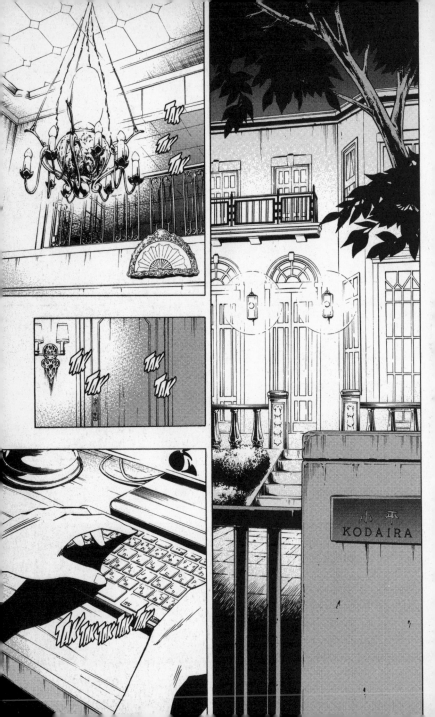

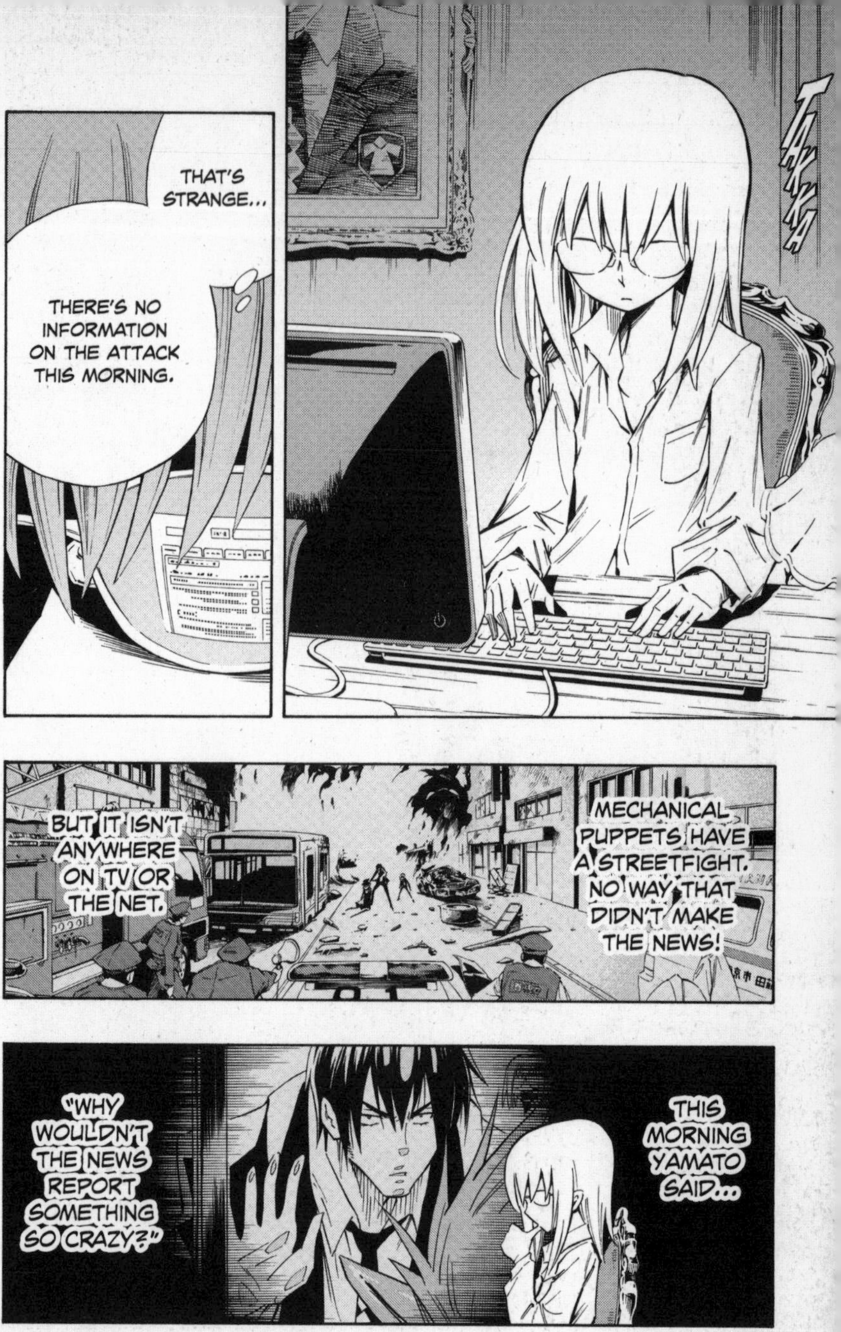
TAKKA
THAT'S STRANGE...
THERE'S NO INFORMATION ON THE ATTACK THIS MORNING.
MECHANICAL PUPPETS HAVE A STREETFIGHT. NO WAY THAT DIDN'T MAKE THE NEWS!
BUT IT ISN'T ANYWHERE ON TV OR THE NET.
THIS MORNING YAMATO SAID...
"WHY WOULDN'T THE NEWS REPORT SOMETHING SO CRAZY?"

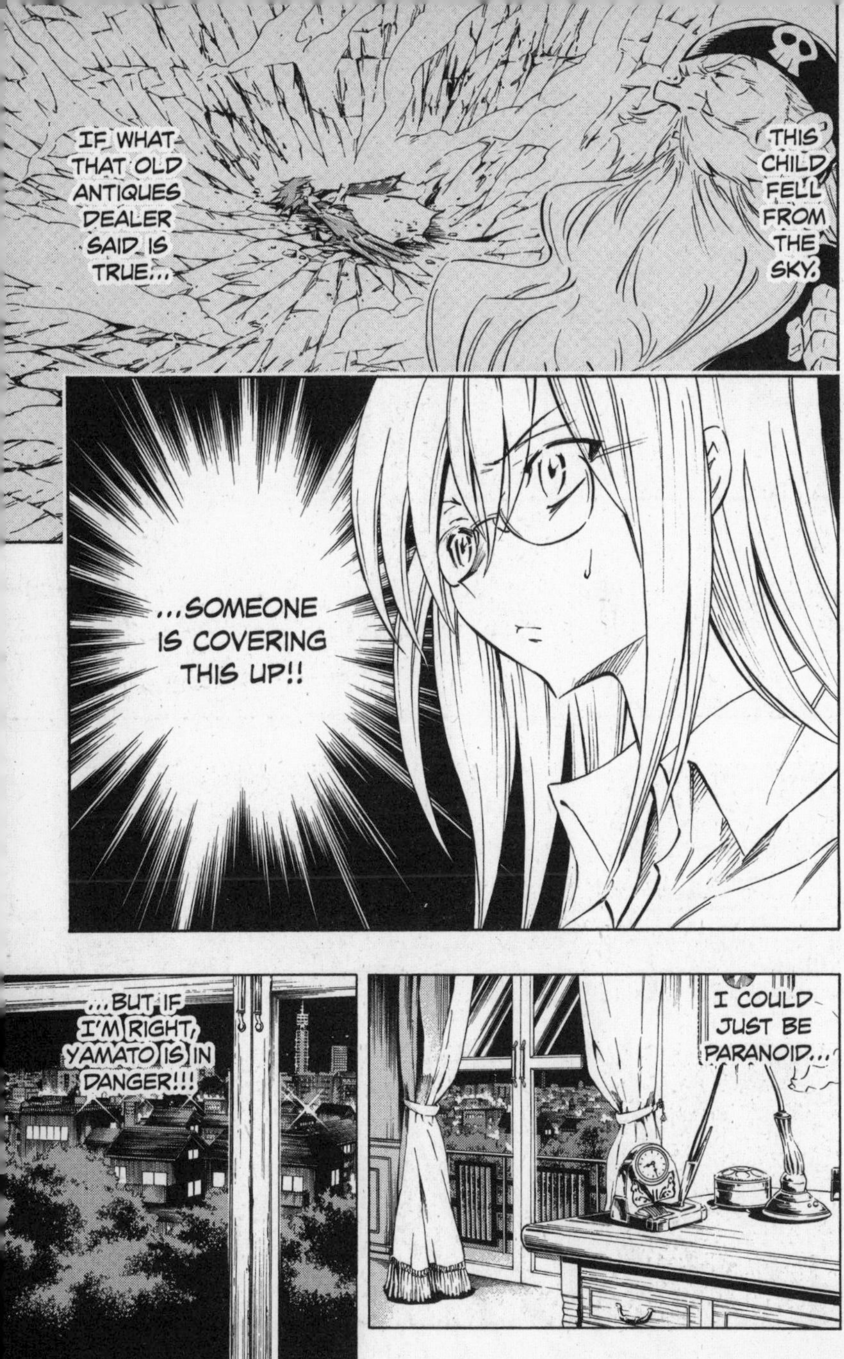
THIS CHILD FELL FROM THE SKY.
IF WHAT THAT OLD ANTIQUES DEALER SAID IS TRUE...
...SOMEONE IS COVERING THIS UP!!
I COULD JUST BE PARANOID...
...BUT IF I'M RIGHT, YAMATO IS IN DANGER!!!

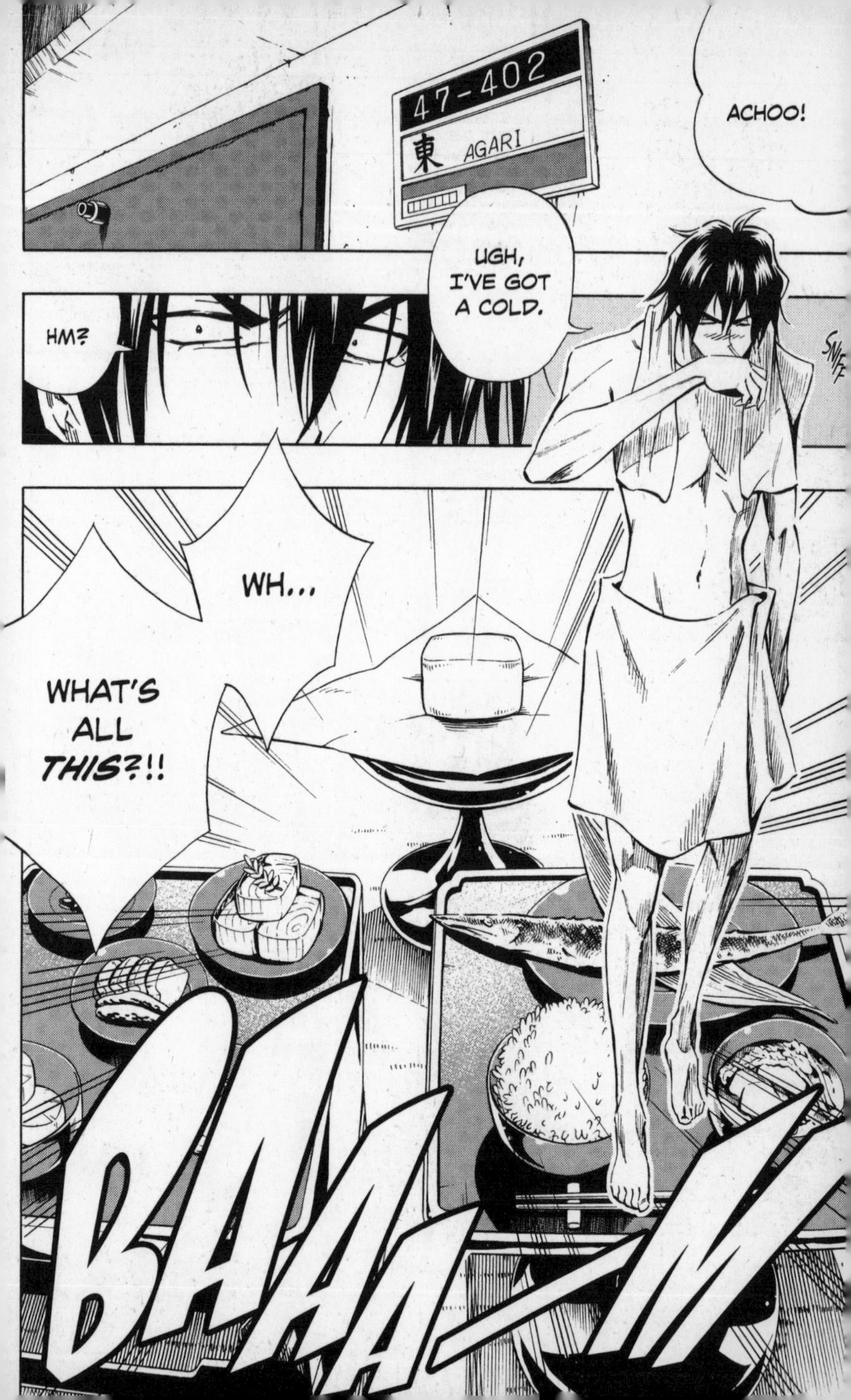
ACHOO!
47-402
東 AGARI
UGH, I'VE GOT A COLD.
SNIFF
HM?
WH...
WHAT'S ALL THIS?!!
BAAA-M

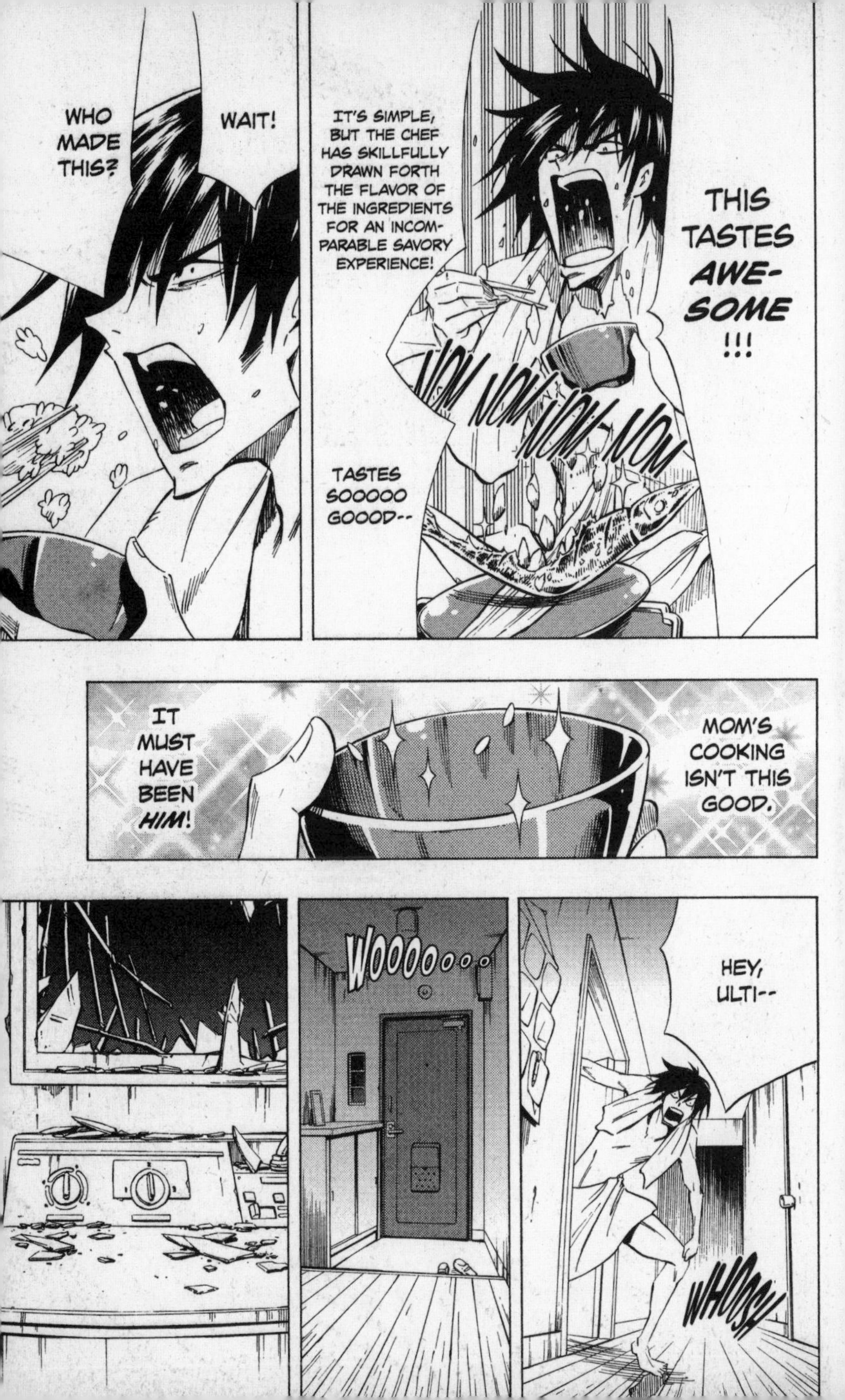
THIS TASTES AWESOME!!!
IT'S SIMPLE, BUT THE CHEF HAS SKILLFULLY DRAWN FORTH THE FLAVOR OF THE INGREDIENTS FOR AN INCOMPARABLE SAVORY EXPERIENCE!
NOM NOM NOM NOM
TASTES SOOOOO GOOOD--
WAIT!
WHO MADE THIS?
MOM'S COOKING ISN'T THIS GOOD.
IT MUST HAVE BEEN HIM!
HEY, ULTI--
WHOOSH
WOOOOooo

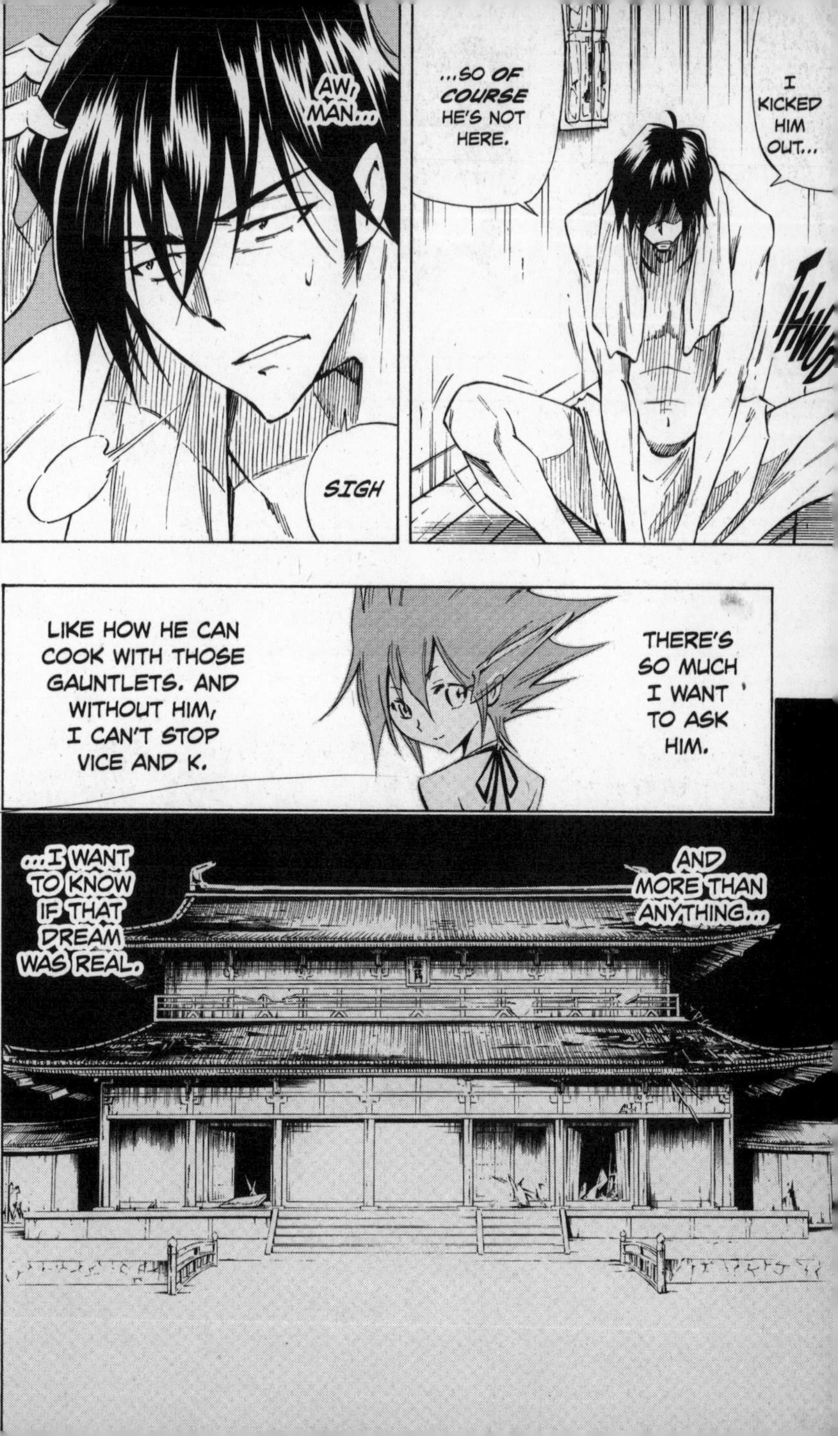
I KICKED HIM OUT...
...SO OF COURSE HE'S NOT HERE.
THWUD
AW, MAN...
SIGH
THERE'S SO MUCH I WANT TO ASK HIM.
LIKE HOW HE CAN COOK WITH THOSE GAUNTLETS. AND WITHOUT HIM, I CAN'T STOP VICE AND K.
AND MORE THAN ANYTHING...
...I WANT TO KNOW IF THAT DREAM WAS REAL.

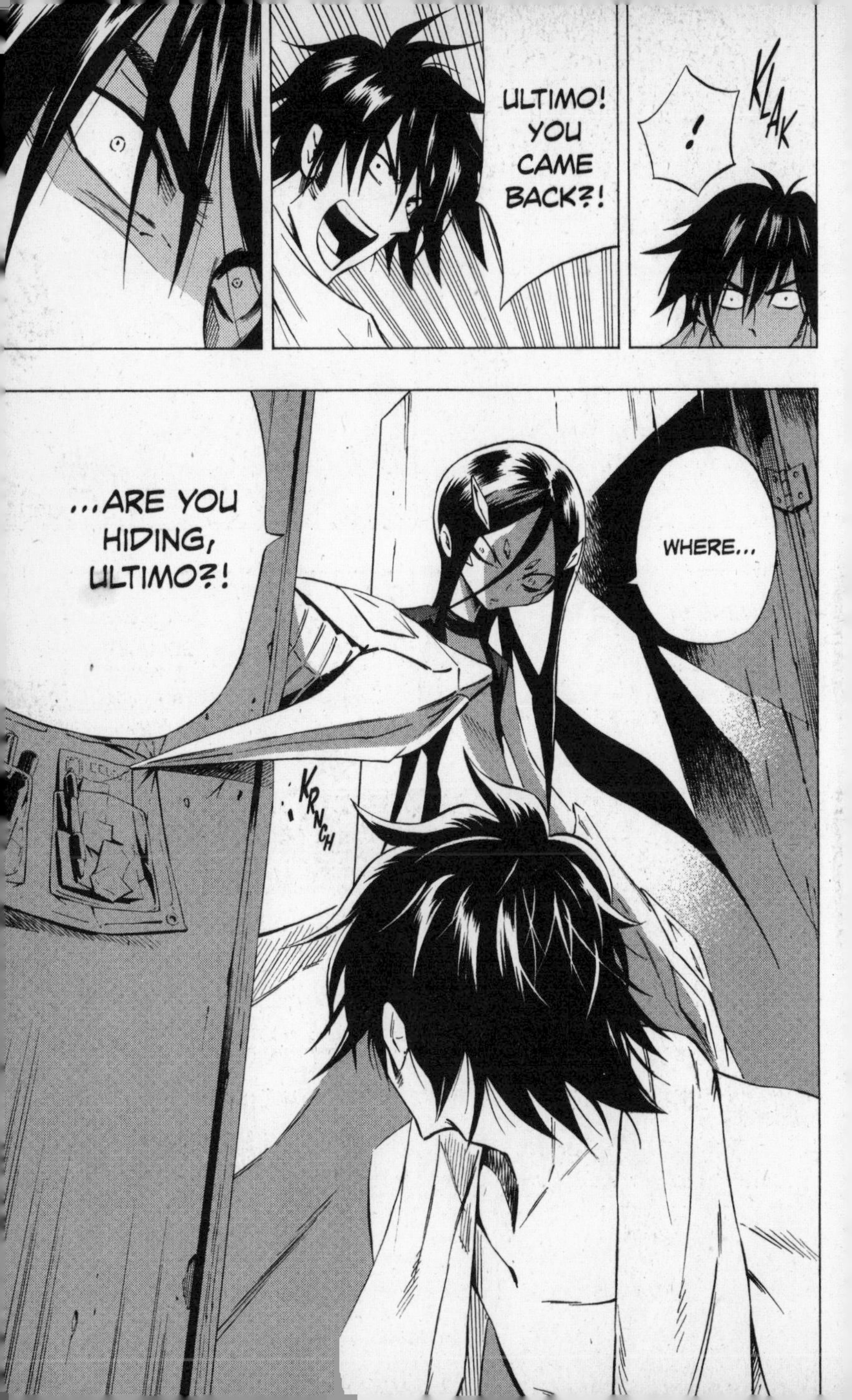
KLAK
!
ULTIMO! YOU CAME BACK?!
WHERE...
...ARE YOU HIDING, ULTIMO?!
KRNCH

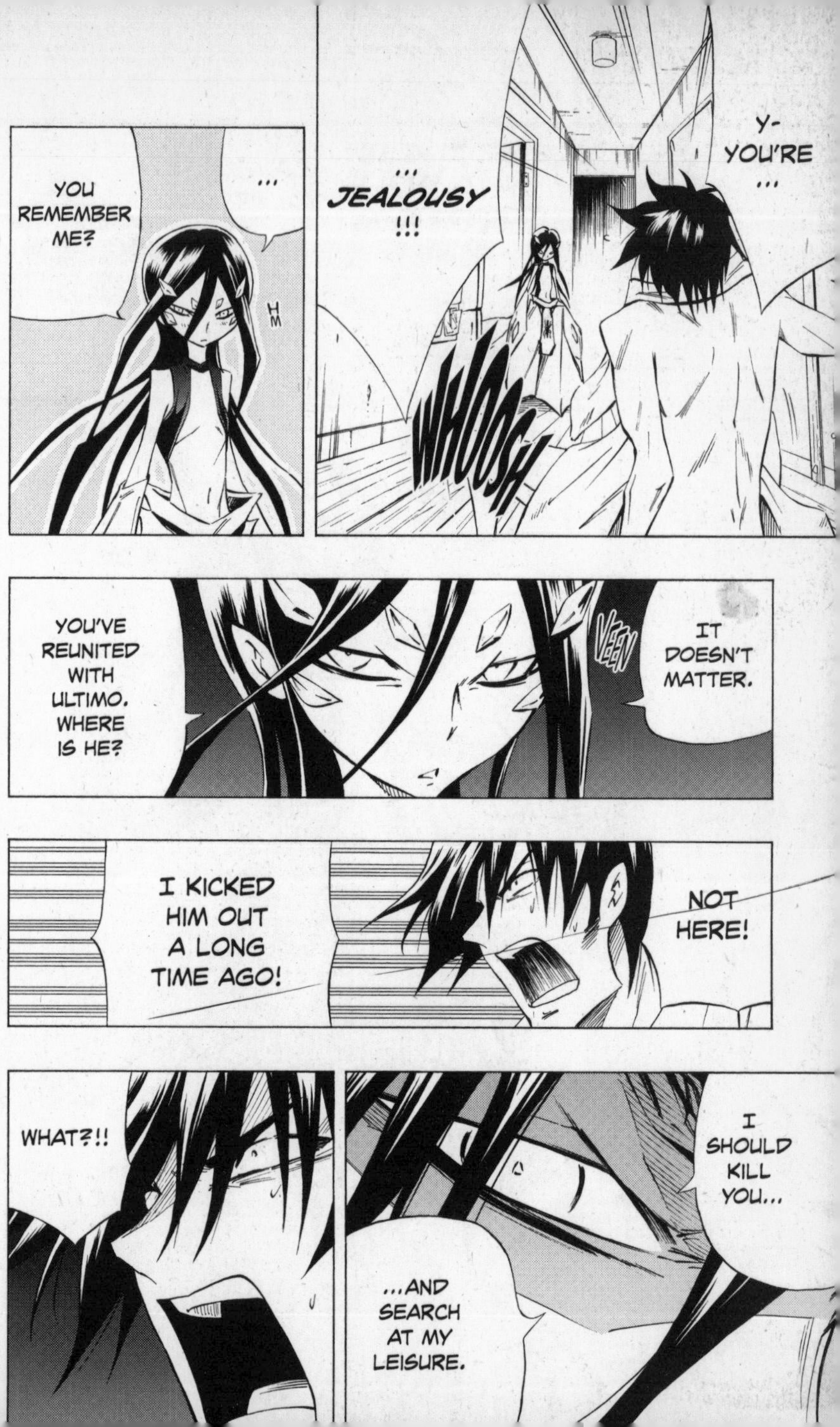
Y- YOU'RE ...
... JEALOUSY !!!
WHOOSH
...
YOU REMEMBER ME?
HM
IT DOESN'T MATTER.
VEEN
YOU'VE REUNITED WITH ULTIMO. WHERE IS HE?
NOT HERE!
I KICKED HIM OUT A LONG TIME AGO!
I SHOULD KILL YOU...
...AND SEARCH AT MY LEISURE.
WHAT?!!

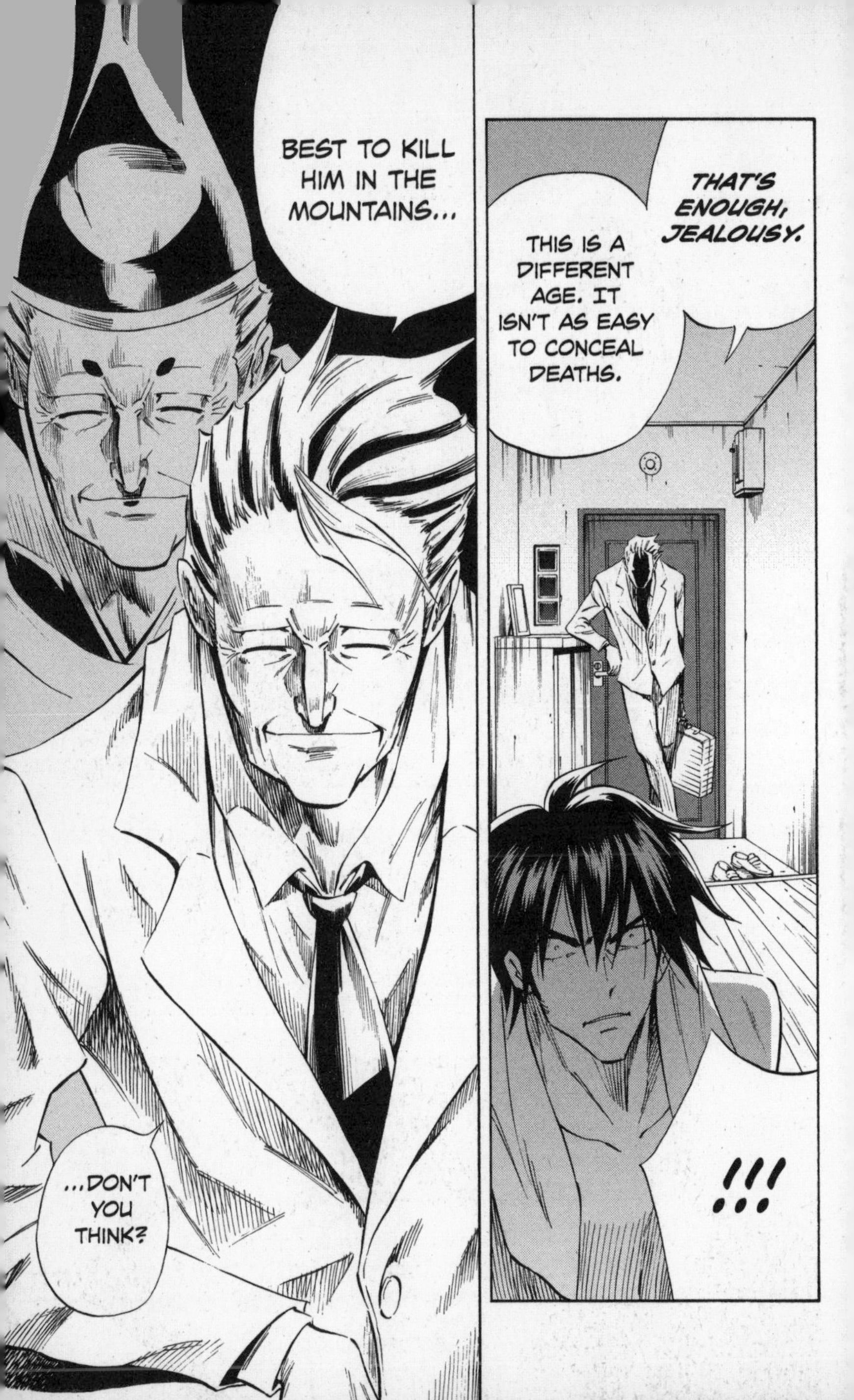
BEST TO KILL HIM IN THE MOUNTAINS...
...DON'T YOU THINK?
THAT'S ENOUGH, JEALOUSY.
THIS IS A DIFFERENT AGE. IT ISN'T AS EASY TO CONCEAL DEATHS.
!!!

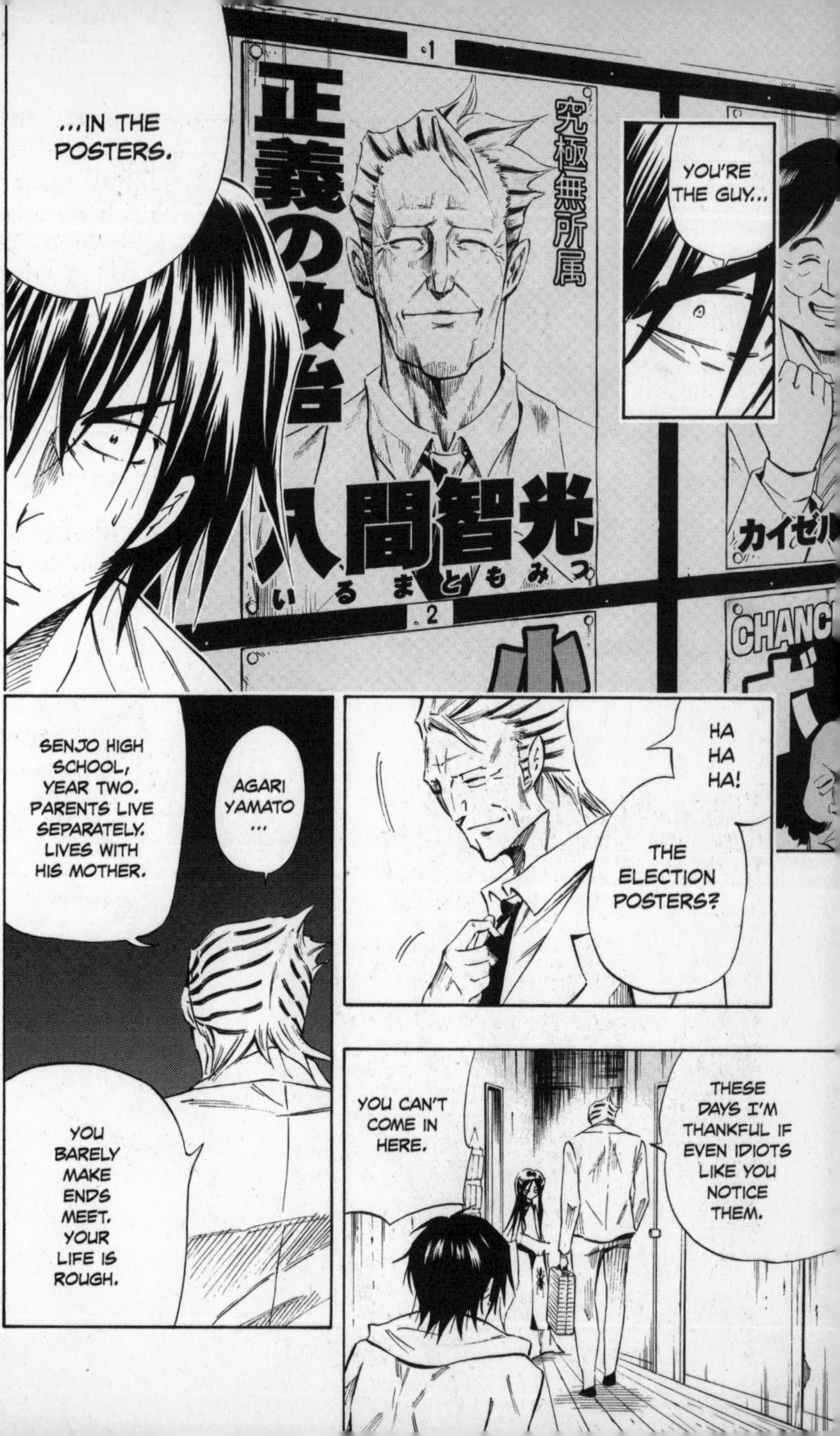
YOU'RE THE GUY...
...IN THE POSTERS.
究極無所属
入間智光
いるまともみつ
HA HA HA!
THE ELECTION POSTERS?
THESE DAYS I'M THANKFUL IF EVEN IDIOTS LIKE YOU NOTICE THEM.
YOU CAN'T COME IN HERE.
AGARI YAMATO ...
SENJO HIGH SCHOOL, YEAR TWO. PARENTS LIVE SEPARATELY. LIVES WITH HIS MOTHER.
YOU BARELY MAKE ENDS MEET. YOUR LIFE IS ROUGH.

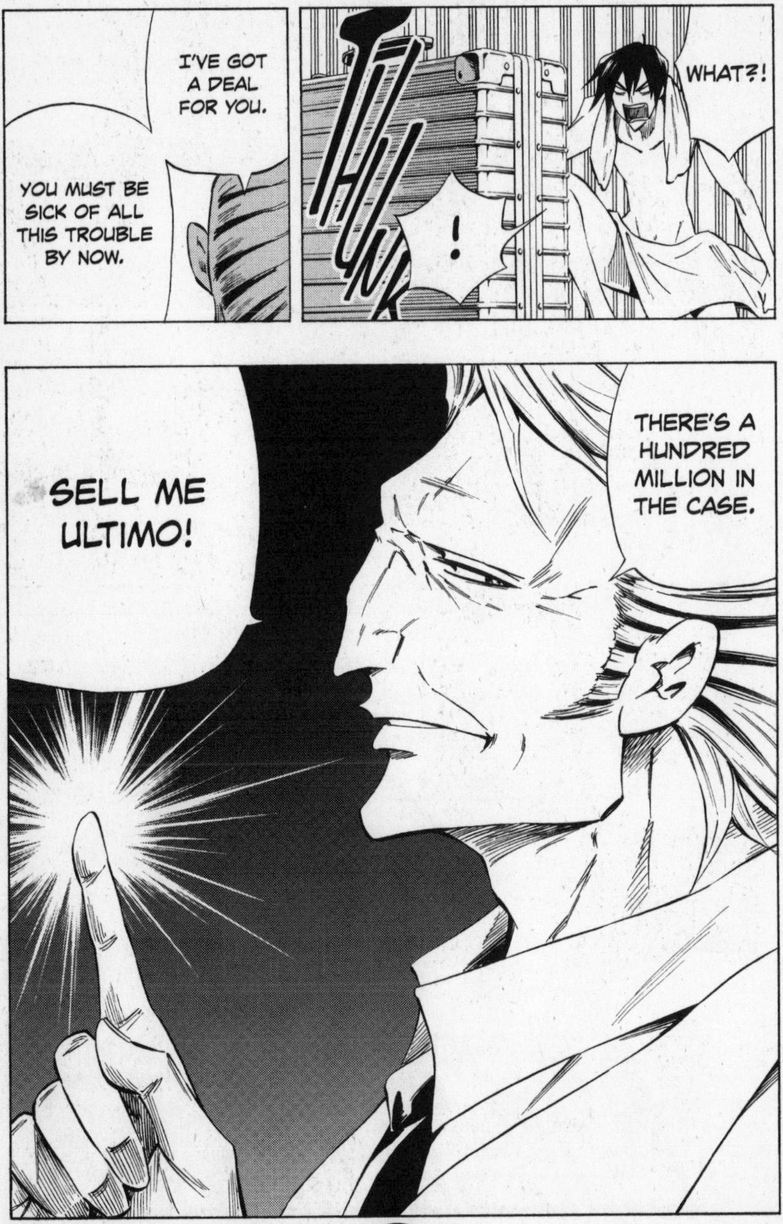
WHAT?!
THUNK
!
I'VE GOT A DEAL FOR YOU.
YOU MUST BE SICK OF ALL THIS TROUBLE BY NOW.
THERE'S A HUNDRED MILLION IN THE CASE.
SELL ME ULTIMO!

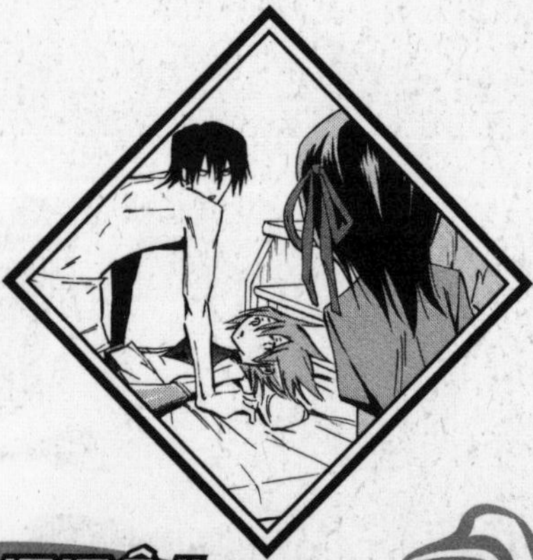

KARAKURIDÔJI
ULTIMO

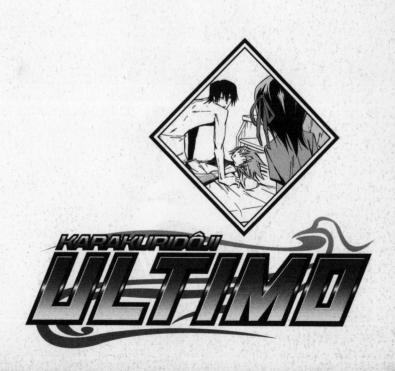

CHARACTER DATA COMPILATION

KARAKURI ILLUSTRATED PROFILES

1

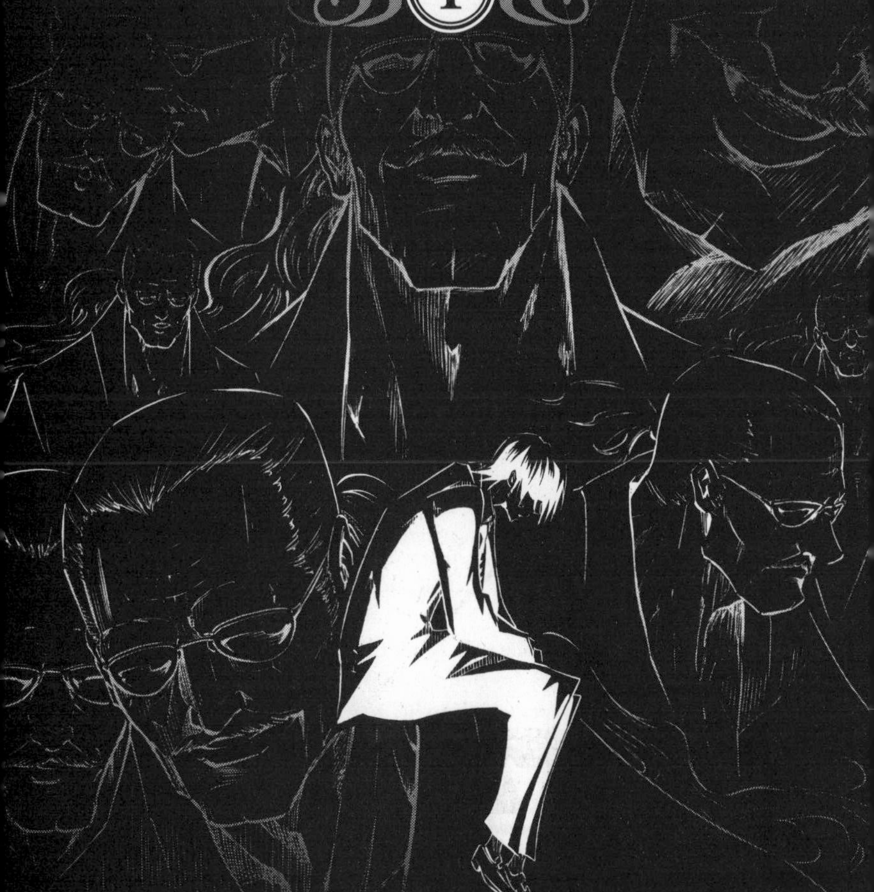

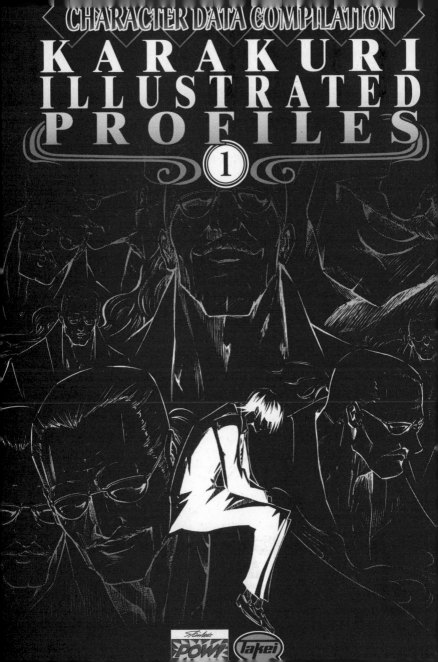

機巧童子とは…その1

機巧童子は人間の「善」と「悪」、そしてそのどちらが
強いのかを知るためにダンスタン博士によって開発された
童子型の機巧人形である。

童子は無垢な者の象徴であり、これが彼らが
純粋な「善」と「悪」であることを示している。これは
同時に彼らが学習型のロボットであることも意味する。

彼らは未完成であり、「殿」と呼ばれる人間を
任意に選出することで共に行動し、時代と地域を
越えたあらゆる人間の「善」と「悪」を学んでいくのだ。

…続く

What is a Karakuri Dôji? Part 1

Mechanical dolls that look like children, the Karakuri Dôji
were designed by Dr. Dunstan to find out about good and evil
from humans—and to discover which is stronger.

Dôji are untainted beings. They can be either pure good or
pure evil. They are robots designed to learn.

But Dôji are incomplete. They must choose a human master
to accompany, in order to acquire the human traits of good
and evil that transcend time and space.

To be continued...

ULTIMO

ウルティモ

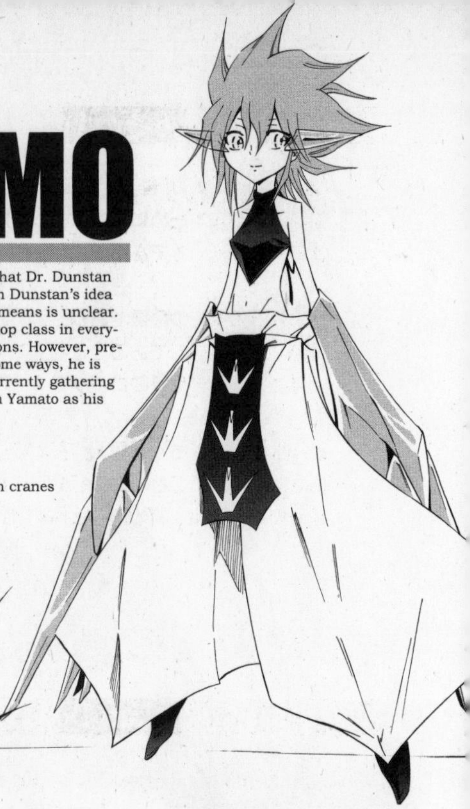

The first Karakuri Dôji of Good that Dr. Dunstan created. His actions are based on Dunstan's idea of "good," but exactly what that means is unclear. Just as his name implies, he is top class in everything from appearance to functions. However, precisely because he is perfect in some ways, he is lacking in many others. He is currently gathering information about goodness with Yamato as his master.

His theme color is scarlet.

His Karakuri Henge are based on cranes and lions.

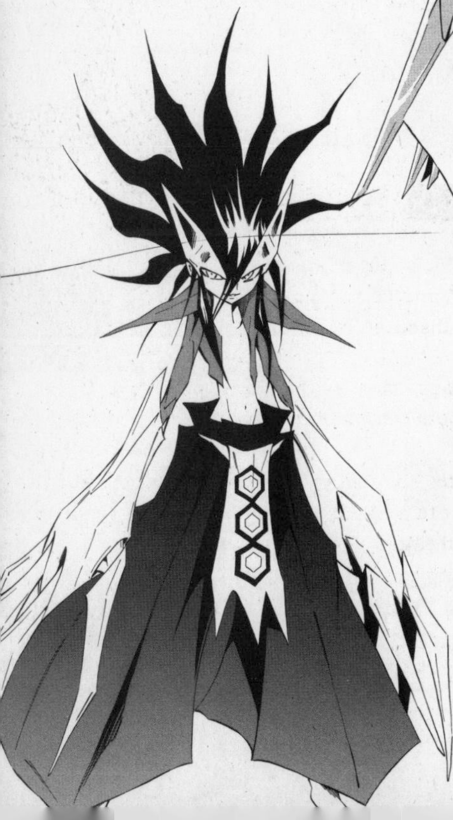

VICE

バイス

The first Karakuri Dôji of Evil, created together with Ultimo. He is a clone possessing the exact same capabilities as Ultimo, but his purpose is the exact opposite. Thus, he bears a name meaning evil. He serves his master in order to learn about evil and gain evil energy, and otherwise acts only under a variety of evil impulses.

His theme color is that of iron. [Usually Vice is associated with green, but here it says his theme color is "iron(or steel)-color."]

His Karakuri Henge are based on turtles and demons.

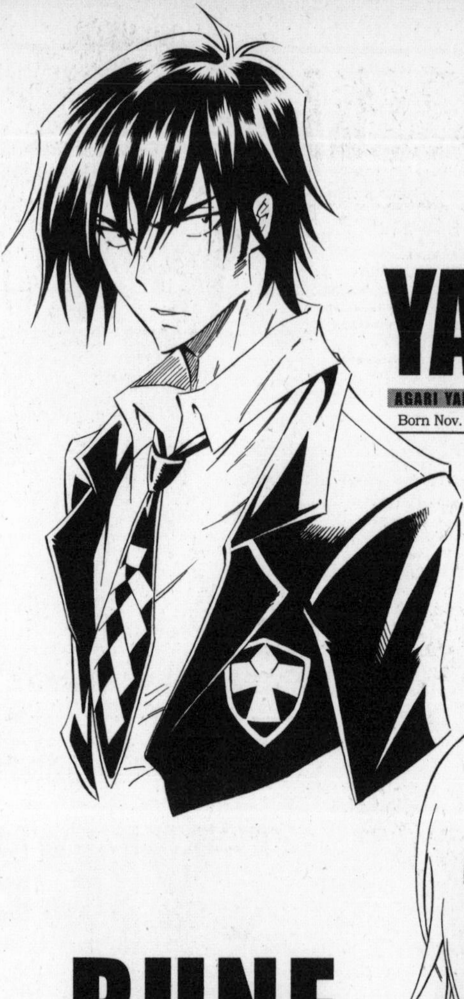

YAMATO

AGARI YAMATO 東大和

Born Nov. 15, Scorpio, Blood type O, 16 years old

The main hero. He is immensely enthusiastic and kind, but always gets himself into trouble. He currently lives with his mother in public housing.

His favorite thing is Sayama.

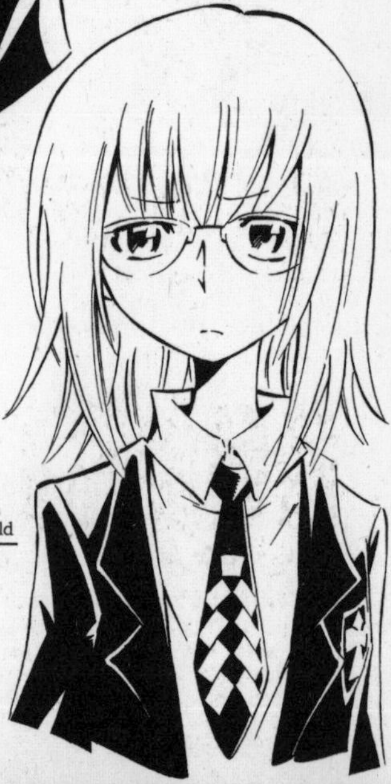

RUNE

小平ルネ KODAIRA RUNE

Born Feb. 4, Aquarius, Blood type AB, 16 years old

A boy in glasses who adores Yamato. His family is rich and he's an excellent student. He's extremely serious, but a little too inflexible. Later on, his character will develop in a surprising way.

His favorite thing is sweets with whipped cream on top.

SAYAMA SAN

狭山 真琴 　SAYAMA MAKOTO

Born May 5, Taurus, Blood type A, 17 years old

A cool and mysterious high school girl who always keeps her head about her. Capable of taking bold action, she has rescued Yamato from crises many times in the past, but her cold reactions deliver even deeper psychological damage.

Her favorite things are mushrooms and cheese.

K

ケー

Born May 31, Gemini, Blood type A, 31 years old

A man in glasses who dreams of being evil. A short-tempered person of low caliber, when he gets flustered he doesn't know what's happening and starts trembling.

His favorite things are motorcycles and heavy metal. He feeds the sparrows on his veranda.

DUNSTAN

ダンスタン

Born Dec. 28, Capricorn, Blood type O, ? years old

Another man in glasses, unidentified and shrouded in mystery. He is a joker-type character who created the Karakuri Dôji, thus giving to the series a wide variety of characters.

His favorite thing is...a secret.

ULTIMO

Volume 1

Original Concept: Stan Lee
Story and Art by: Hiroyuki Takei

SHONEN JUMP Manga Edition

This graphic novel contains material that was originally published in English in SHONEN JUMP #79-82
Artwork in the magazine may have been slightly altered from that presented here.

Translation | John Werry
Series Touch-up Art & Lettering | James Gaubatz
Design | Fawn Lau
Series Editor | Joel Enos
Graphic Novel Editor | Jann Jones

VP, Production | Alvin Lu
VP, Sales & Product Marketing | Gonzalo Ferreyra
VP, Creative | Linda Espinosa
Publisher | Hyoe Narita

RATED T FOR TEEN

PARENTAL ADVISORY
ULTIMO is rated T for Teen and is recommended for ages 13 and up. This volume contains fantasy violence.
ratings.viz.com

Printed in the U.S.A.

Published by VIZ Media, LLC
P.O. Box 77010
San Francisco, CA 94107

10 9 8 7 6 5 4 3 2 1
First printing, February 2010

www.viz.com

www.shonenjump.com

STAN LEE

As a kid, Stanley Martin Lieber spent a lot of time dreaming up wild adventures. By the time he got to high school, he was putting his imagination to work writing stories at Timely, a publishing company that went on to become the legendary Marvel Comics. Starting with the *Fantastic Four*, Lee and his partner Jack Kirby created just about every superhero you can think of, including *Spider-Man*, the *X-Men*, the *Hulk*, *Iron Man*, *Daredevil* and *Thor*. Along the way, he wrote under a lot of pen names, but the one that stuck was Stan Lee.

HIROYUKI TAKEI

Unconventional author/artist Hiroyuki Takei began his career by winning the coveted Hop Step Award (for new manga artists) and the Osamu Tezuka Cultural Prize (named after the famous artist of the same name). After working as an assistant to famed artist Nobuhiro Watsuki, Takei debuted in *Weekly Shonen Jump* in 1997 with *Butsu Zone*, an action series based on Buddhist mythology. His multicultural adventure manga *Shaman King*, which debuted in 1998, became a hit and was adapted into an anime TV series. Takei lists Osamu Tezuka, American comics and robot anime among his many influences.

HIROYUKI TAKEI

STAN LEE

CREATOR INTERVIEW

HIROYUKI TAKEI: How did you come up with the ideas for Ultimo?

STAN LEE: I don't know. I was trying to do something that would be good for the Japanese audience as well as an American audience. There aren't too many robots here in America. I didn't know if they had a good robot fighting the bad ones in Japan and thought maybe this idea would be good for both countries. So I said, "Well, why not? I'll write it, and we'll see what they say." When I saw your first drawings, they made me think of many new things. I got so excited about them that I was really thrilled to be working with an artist like you.

HK: What made you want to collaborate with a Japanese manga and comic artist?

SL: I love Japanese manga, and I know how popular it is, certainly in Japan, but even in America. I've never done anything with manga. I don't like to think there is anything that I haven't done, so I was really eager to do something, and to do it with the best artist possible. That was, you know, something I couldn't resist.

HK: You have the rough page layouts. What did you think when you first saw them?

SL: It's very hard for me to understand them because storyboards in America look a little different. They're tighter and they're more complete. The Japanese layouts are very rough, so it's gonna take me a while to get used to looking at that type of storyboard. Of course, I need English to understand what I'm looking at. It's a little hard to tell because I don't read Japanese as well as I used to. [*Laughter*]

HK: Stick figures are actually what it come down to because we have to produce 1 pages a week.

SL: That's a tremendous amount. I mean when I was doing comic books years ago our books were originally 64 pages in the 1930s. Then they got whittled down to 4 pages, and finally by the 60s they were only 32 pages. Now, of the 32 pages, 8 or so wer ads. There ended up being about 20 or 2 pages of actual comics, and we had to do that in a month. For you people to do all o this in one week, I think that is absolutely amazing. And to have it turn out as good a it does, I think you're all geniuses.

HK: Everyone does it in Japan.

SL: No wonder you always look so tired The difference is, we only did 20 pages month, but I was writing between 12 and 20 comic books a month. So we did quite a lo too. You know, there was Spider-Man, Th Hulk, The X-Men and so on.

HK: What do you think of Japanese manga

SL: I love it! That's why I wanted to do this I love the way the stories flow. I love th characters. I love everything about it. I jus hope that I can write it as well as what I'v read in Japanese manga. But I'm gonna d my best.

HK: Lastly, do you have a message fo SHONEN JUMP readers?

SL: Oh, absolutely. Save your mone and go out there and buy as many copie of *Ultimo* as you possibly can. Don't jus buy one, because they're gonna be worth lot of money in the future. So buy a lot o them and save them. Now, I have a questio for you. Why are you sitting here wastin all this time when you should be workin on *Ultimo* and getting that out as fast a possible?! [*Laughter*]

IN THE NEXT VOLUME...

Things just keep getting more complicated for Yamato since Ultimo showed up. Now Yamato and Ultimo must face new Dôji and deal with people whose intentions aren't always so clear. Can Yamato find the strength to meet these challenges and solve the mysteries of the Karakuri Dôji?

AVAILABLE AUGUST 2010!
Read it first in SHONEN JUMP magazine!

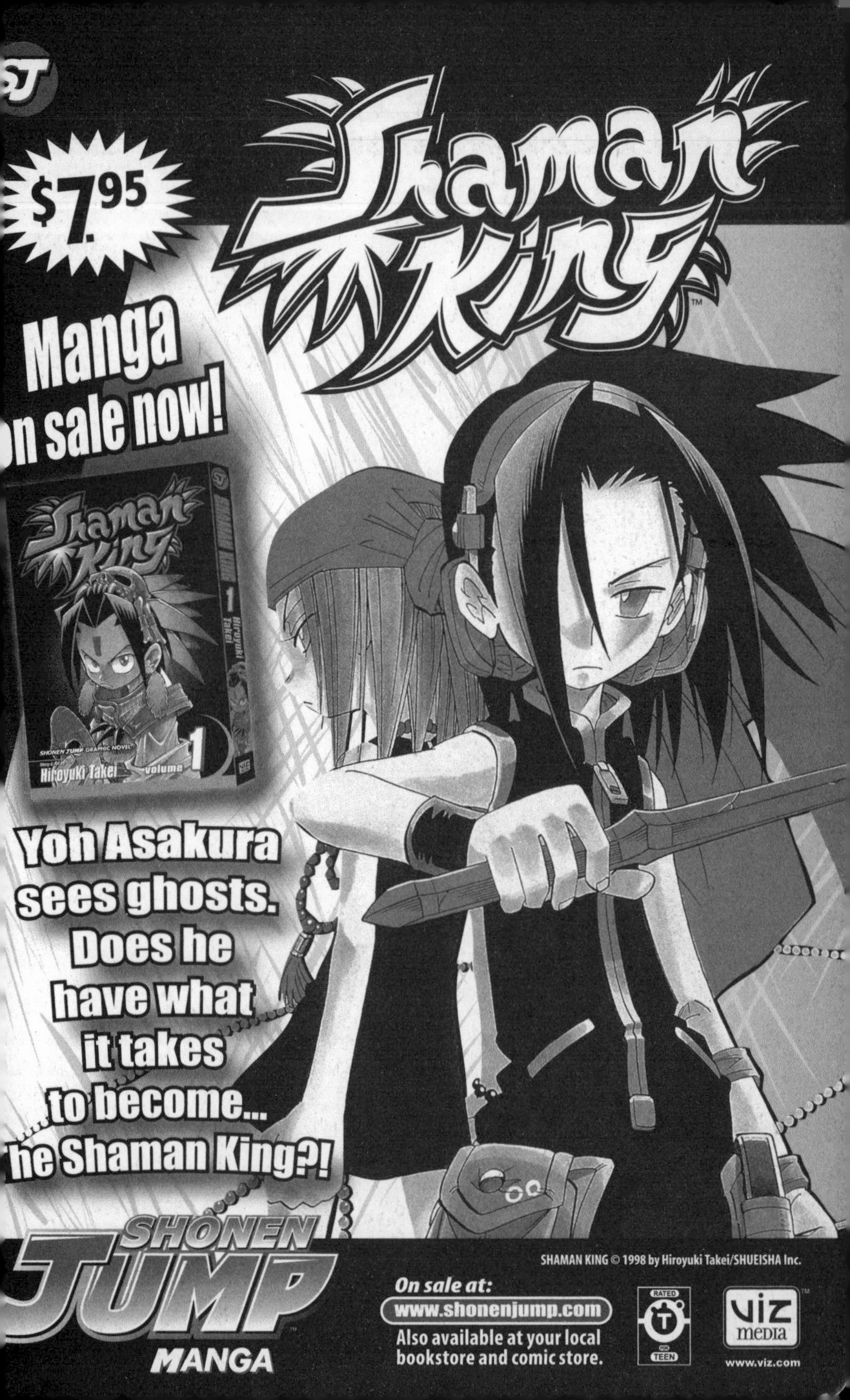